ART OF INTERVIEW

ARVIND UPADHYAY

Contents

Preface   *v*

  1. You Are In Charge   1

  2. The Interview Process   9

  3. Who Are You?   26

  4. So, Tell Me About Yourself   33

  5. Questions About Your Education   45

  6. Questions About Your Experience   52

  7. Questions About Core Competencies   68

  8. Questions About Your Current (or Last) Job   77

  9. So Why Us?   87

10. Questions About Your Personal Life   99

11. Questions To Wrap Things Up   111

Preface

To a large degree, the success of your interview will depend on your ability to discover needs and empathize with the interviewer. You can do this by asking questions that verify your understanding of what the interviewer has just said, without editorializing or expressing an opinion. By establishing empathy in this manner, you'll be in a better position to freely exchange ideas, and demonstrate your suitability for the job.

In addition to empathy, there are four other intangible fundamentals to a successful interview. These intangibles will influence the way your personality is perceived, and will affect the degree of rapport, or personal chemistry you'll share with the employer.

Enthusiasm — Leave no doubt as to your level of interest in the job. You may think it's unnecessary to do this, but employers often choose the more enthusiastic candidate in the case of a two-way tie. Besides, it's best to keep your options open — wouldn't you rather be in a position to turn down an offer, than have a prospective job evaporate from your grasp by giving a lethargic interview?

Technical interest — Employers look for people who love what they do, and get excited by the prospect of tearing into the nitty-gritty of the job.

Confidence — No one likes a braggart, but the candidate who's sure of his or her abilities will almost certainly be more favorably received.

Intensity — The last thing you want to do is come across as "flat" in your interview. There's nothing inherently wrong with being a laid back person; but sleepwalkers rarely get hired.

By the way, most employers are aware of how stressful it can be to interview for a new position, and will do everything they can to put you at ease.

Since interviewing also involves the exchange of tangible information, make sure to:

Present your background in a thorough and accurate manner;

Gather data concerning the company, the industry, the position, and the specific opportunity;

Link your abilities with the company needs in the mind of the employer; and

Build a strong case for why the company should hire you, based on the discoveries you make from building rapport and asking the right questions.

Both for your sake and the employer's, never leave an interview without exchanging fundamental information. The more you know about each other, the more potential you'll have for establishing rapport, and making an informed decision.

There are two ways to answer interview questions: the short version and the long version. When a question is open-ended, I always suggest to candidates that they say, "Let me give you the short version. If we need to explore some aspect of the answer more fully, I'd be happy to go into greater depth, and give you the long version."

The reason you should respond this way is because it's often difficult to know what type of answer each question will need. A question like, "What was your most difficult assignment?" might take anywhere from thirty seconds to thirty minutes to answer, depending on the detail you choose to give.

Therefore, you must always remember that the interviewer's the one who asked the question. So you should tailor your answer to what he or she needs to know, without a lot of extraneous rambling or superfluous explanation. Why waste time and create a negative impression by giving a sermon when a short prayer would do just fine?

Let's suppose you were interviewing for a sales management position, and the interviewer asked you, "What sort of sales experience have you had in the past?"

Well, that's exactly the sort of question that can get you into trouble if you don't use the short version/long version method. Most people would just start rattling off everything in their memory that relates to their sales experience. Though the information might be useful to the interviewer, your answer could get pretty complicated and long-winded unless it's neatly packaged.

One way to answer the question might be, "I've held sales positions with three different consumer product companies over a nine-year period. Where would you like me to start?"

Or, you might simply say, "Let me give you the short version first, and you can tell me where you want to go into more depth. I've had nine years experience in consumer product sales with three different companies, and held the titles of district, regional, and national sales manager. What aspect of my background would you like to concentrate on?"

By using this method, you telegraph to the interviewer that your thoughts are well organized, and that you want to understand the intent of the question before you travel too far in a direction neither of you wants to go. After you get the green light, you can spend your interviewing time discussing in detail the things that are important, not whatever happens to pop into your mind.

I've got a friend who's the hiring manager of an electronics company. He told me once that he brought a candidate into his office to make him a job offer. An hour later, the candidate left. I asked my friend if he had hired the candidate.

"No," he said. "I tried. But the candidate wouldn't stop talking long enough for me to make him an offer."

Don't misinterpret me. I'm not suggesting that an interview should consist of a series of monosyllabic grunts. It's just that nothing turns off an employer faster than a windbag candidate.

By using the short version/long version method to answer questions, you'll never talk yourself out of a job.

Beware: An interview will quickly disintegrate into an interrogation or monologue unless you ask some high quality questions of your own. Candidate questions are the lifeblood of any successful interview, because they:

Create dialogue, which will not only enable the two of you to learn more about each other, but will help you visualize what it'll be like working together once you've been hired;

Clarify your understanding of the company and the position responsibilities;

Indicate your grasp of the fundamental issues discussed so far;

Reveal your ability to probe beyond the superficial; and

Challenge the employer to reveal his or her own depth of knowledge, or commitment to the job.

Your questions should always be slanted in such a way as to show empathy, interest, or understanding of the employer's needs. After all, the reason you're interviewing is because the employer's company has some piece of work which needs to be completed, or a problem that needs correcting. Here are some questions that have proven to be very effective:

What's the most important issue facing your department?

How can I help you accomplish this objective?

How long has it been since you first identified this need?

How long have you been trying to correct it?

Have you tried using your present staff to get the job done? What was the result?

What other means have you used? For example, have you brought in independent contractors, or temporary help, or employees borrowed from other departments? Or have you recently hired people who haven't worked out?

Is there any particular skill or attitude you feel is critical to getting the job done?

Is there a unique aspect of my background that you'd like to exploit in order to help accomplish your objectives?

Questions like these will not only give you a sense of the company's goals and priorities, they'll indicate to the interviewer your concern for satisfying the company's objectives.

Here are seven of the most commonly asked interviewing questions. Do yourself and the prospective employer a favor, and give them some thought before the interview occurs.

Why do you want this job?

Why do you want to leave your present company?

Where do you see yourself in five years?

What are your personal goals?

What are your strengths? Weaknesses?

What do you like most about your current company?

What do you like least about your current company?

The last question is probably the hardest to answer: What do you like least about your present company?

I've found that rather than pointing out the faults of other people ("I can't stand the office politics," or, "I don't get along with my boss"), it's best to place the burden on yourself ("I feel I'm ready to exercise a new set of professional muscles," or, "The type of technology I'm interested in isn't available to me now.").

By answering in this manner, you'll avoid pointing the finger at someone else, or coming across as a whiner or complainer. It does no good to speak negatively about others.

I suggest you think through the answers to the above questions for two reasons.

First, it won't help your chances any to hem and haw over fundamental issues such as these. (The answers you give to these types of questions should be no-brainers.)

And secondly, the questions will help you evaluate your career choices before spending time and energy on an interview. If you don't feel comfortable with the answers you come up with, maybe the new job isn't right for you.

There's a good chance you'll be asked about your current and expected level of compensation. Here's the way to handle the following questions:

What are you currently earning?Answer: "My compensation, including bonus, is in the high-forties. I'm expecting my annual review next month, and that should put me in the low-fifties."

What sort of money would you need in order to come to work for our company?Answer: "I feel that the opportunity is the most important issue, not salary. If we decide to work together, I'm sure you'll make me a fair offer."

Notice the way a range was given as the answer to question [1], not a specific dollar figure. However, if the interviewer presses for a exact answer, then by all means, be precise, in terms of salary, bonus, benefits, expected increase, and so forth.

In answer to question [2], if the interviewer tries to zero in on your expected compensation, you should also suggest a range, as in, "I would need something in the low- to mid- fifties." Getting locked in to an exact figure may work against you later, in one of two ways: either the number you give is lower than you really want to accept; or the number appears too high or too low to the employer, and an offer never comes. By using a range, you can keep your options open.

There are four types of questions that interviewers like to ask.

Resume questions require accurate, objective answers, since your resume consists of facts which tend to be quantifiable (and verifiable). Try to avoid answers which exaggerate your achievements, or appear to be opinionated, vague, or egocentric.

Second, interviewers will usually want you to comment on your abilities, or assess your past performance. They'll ask self-appraisal questions like, "What do you think is your greatest asset?" or, "Can you tell me something you've done that was very creative?"

Third, interviewers like to know how you respond to different stimuli. Situation questions ask you to explain certain actions you took in the past, or require that you explore hypothetical scenarios that may occur in the future. "How would you stay profitable during a recession?" or, "How would you go about laying off 1300 employees?" or, "How would you handle customer complaints if the company drastically raised its prices?" are typical situation questions.

And lastly, some employers like to test your mettle with stress questions such as, "After you die, what would you like your epitaph to read?" or, "If you were to compare yourself to any U.S. president, who would it be?" or, "It's obvious your background makes you totally unqualified for this position. Why should we even waste our time talking?"

Stress questions are designed to evaluate your emotional reflexes, creativity, or attitudes while you're under pressure. Since off-the-wall or confrontational questions tend to jolt your equilibrium, or put you in a defensive posture, the best way to handle them is to stay calm and give carefully considered answers.

Whenever I hear a stress question, I immediately think of the Miss Universe beauty pageant. The finalists (usually sheltered teenagers from places like Zambia or Uruguay) are asked before a live television audience of three and a half billion people to give heartfelt and earnest responses to incongruous questions like, "What would you tell the leaders of all the countries on earth to do to promote world peace?"

Of course, your sense of humor will come in handy during the entire interviewing process, just so long as you don't go over the edge. I heard of a candidate once who, when asked to describe his ideal job, replied, "To have beautiful women rub my back with hot oil." Needless to say, he wasn't hired.

Even if it were possible to anticipate every interview question, memorizing dozens of stock answers would be impractical, to say the least. The best policy is to review your background, your priorities, and your reasons for considering a new position; and to handle the interview as honestly as you can. If you don't know the answer to a question, just say so, or ask for a moment to think about your response.

At the conclusion of your interview, you can wrap up any unfinished business you failed to cover so far, and begin to explore the future of your candidacy.

During your interview wrap-up, it's a good practice to make the interviewer aware of other opportunities you're exploring, as long as they're genuine, and their timing has some bearing on your own decision making.

The fact that you're actively exploring other opportunities may affect the speed with which the company makes its hiring decision. It may even positively influence the eventual outcome, since the company may want to act quickly so as not to lose you.

However, your other activity should be presented in the spirit of assistance to the interviewer, not as a thinly veiled threat or negotiating tactic. I'd advise you to play it straight with the interviewer.

And remember to maintain a positive attitude. In today's job market, you'd be surprised how often victory is snatched from the jaws of defeat.

The better your interviewing skills, the greater your chances of getting the job.

1

You Are in Charge

Unemployment figures and pundits paint a contrasting picture— while the job market for current or recent college grads is considered the best in a decade or more, there are 6.5 million people "working part time for economic reasons." In other words, 6.5 million people who would prefer to work full time but can't find a full-time job. Whether we are in a booming economy or a recession, most of the things you need to know and do during the interview process do not really change. In the 27 years since I wrote the first edition, an ever-changing job market has morphed from a seller's (employee-friendly) market to a buyer's (employer-friendly) market and back again. But in good times and bad, the power this book has given interviewees—whatever their ages, skills, or qualifications—has continued to grow.

I certainly couldn't boast of my own interviewing skills before I wrote this book. On the contrary, I had often not gotten jobs for which I was eminently qualified. So I spent quite a lot of time learning all the mistakes you could possibly make, having made each one of them—twice. Now, as a veteran of the other side of the desk as well (I've hired hundreds and interviewed thousands), I can tell you that interviewing is more serious business than ever before. Employers are looking for "self-managing" employees—people who are versatile, confident, ready and able to work with a team, and not afraid to roll up their sleeves, work long hours, and get the job done. "That's me," you chortle. Congratulations. But you won't get the chance to prove yourself on the job without making it through the interview process. You can't cheat on these tests There has been one significant development since the last edition of this book. According to the Wall Street Journal, hundreds of companies—including 457 of the Fortune

500—are using some form of "personality" testing that aims to correlate specific personality traits with success in a particular job. One test vendor, Infor, claims to assess more than a million candidates a month. While tests such as Myers-Briggs and the MMPI (Minnesota Multiphasic Personality Inventory) were popular during the 1960s and '70s, we are clearly in a new age that Time magazine recently noted "is being driven by a collision of two hot trends: Big Data and analytics...The result is a mostly unchallenged belief that lots of data combined with lots of analytics can optimize pretty much anything...even people. Hence, people analytics." You may now have to take the DISC Assessment, which will grade you in four areas—Dominance, Defiance, Steadiness, and Conscientiousness. Or the Hogan Personality Inventory, which assesses five. The 16PF measures 16 "normal-range" personality traits and five "second-order" traits. The California Psychological Inventory uses 18 scales in four classes to determine what the test taker will do in specific on-the-job situations. And the Caliper Profile will assess 25 personality traits related to job performance. The winner of this personality numbers game so far is Gallup's Clifton Strengthfinder, which measures 34 traits (but is most interested in your top five). I know from experience that you cannot "beat" these tests. If you try to choose the answers you believe are "obviously" the ones showing your leadership, motivational, or team-building skills, you will not succeed. Since you can't really prepare for these tests, relax and try to answer the questions honestly. Most such tests are merely trying to identify the jobs for which your "personality type" is best suited. And at most companies, they are merely one component of the interview process. I will leave it to others to argue whether it is possible (or desirable) to accurately test for job-specific "success traits." Whatever you believe about this new trend, it is clearly another obstacle many of you will need to hurdle. Interviewing was never easy, and right now it is as hard as ever. Companies are taking far longer to make hiring decisions, and only after subjecting prospective employees to these tests and scheduling more and longer interviews. But of all the tools in your professional arsenal, your ability to shine in that brief moment in time—your initial interview— can make or break your chances for a second go-around, and, ultimately, dictate whether you're even given a shot at the job. Practice still makes perfect Like playing the piano, interviewing takes practice, and practice makes perfect. The hours of personal interviewing experience— the tragedies and the triumphs—as well as my years as an interviewer are the basis for this book. I hope to spare you many of the indignities I suffered along the way, by helping you prepare for the interview of your worst nightmares—at a comfortable remove from the interviewer's glare.

Will you have to answer every question I've included? Certainly not—at least, not in a single interview. But chances are, the questions tomorrow's interviewer doesn't ask will be on the tip of the next interviewer's tongue. Why? It's a mystery. I didn't realize 25 years ago that I would start a competitive publishing battle to see how many interview questions could be featured in a single book. There were always more than 101 questions in my book once one considered all the variations that I listed. But the success of that first edition led to an unfortunate numbers game. Soon there was a book touting 201 questions and answers, then 301, then 500, and, in a final burst of oneupmanship, 501. These numbers really don't matter, especially if a single word change in one question magically transforms it into another. So please don't count the questions in this edition or worry that you need to look at these other books to get a more "complete" list. Believe me, the ones in this book will suffice! Become an interview artist Most interviewers are not trying to torture you for sport. Their motive is to quickly learn enough about you to make an informed decision—should you stay or should you go? By the same token, if you know what they're looking for, you can craft your answers accordingly (and reduce your own fear and anxiety at the same time). I hope you'll take it a step further and use these questions as the basis for some thoughtful self-exploration. You'll need to be prepared to think for yourself—on your feet, not by the seat of your pants. While it is certainly competitive, the interview process is not a competition. Rather than thinking of yourself as an athlete trying to "out-answer" the other candidates, consider an interview your chance to be an artist—to paint a portrait of the person you are, the candidate any company should like, respect...and want to hire .

Chapters 1 and 2 offer a detailed discussion of the work you need to do and the things you need to think about long before you strut into your first interview. Interviewing may not be 99 percent preparation, but it's certainly 50 percent. In Chapters 3 through 10, we'll get into the meat of the book—the questions for which you must prepare and the answers most interviewers are hoping to hear. Each question is generally followed by one or more subheadings: What do they want to hear? (What information is the interviewer seeking?) Thumbs Up (What's a good answer?) Thumbs Down (What's a poor answer?) I've listed the follow-up questions you should expect or variations an interviewer may substitute after many of the questions. The questions in this book are grouped by type; they are not in some suggested order. Many of the questions in chapters 8 or 10, for example, may well be some of the first questions asked in every interview! So read the entire book and prepare for all of the questions in any order. Despite the emphasis on "great answers," I do not recommend rote memorization. Trotting out a staged, "textbook" answer to a question is not the point of the interview process... or of this book. It is actually more important to concentrate on the "What do they want to hear?" section after each question, to have an understanding of why the interviewer is asking a particular question and what you need to do to frame a winning answer. The "thumbs down" after many of the questions indicate answers that will make the average interviewer cringe and the busy interviewer simply suggest you try another firm.

Oh, no, you didn't! I'm going to assume that you have already been on enough interviews (or, if you're a recent graduate, read enough interviewing books), to know that there are rules to follow during interviews. So I'm not going to discuss most of them here. But there is a list of "no-no's" that are so important, failing to avoid them can virtually doom any chance you have of securing the job before the interview even starts. Given their seriousness, I thought it prudent to remind you of them: "What does this company do?" A key part of the interview process is preparation—researching the company, industry, and position, preparing pertinent questions, being ready to sprinkle your knowledge into the conversation. So failing to do any of this will not impress most interviewers. I have had candidates ask me what exactly my company did. The immediate and obvious answer: Not hire them. On time and looking good For many interviewers, showing up late is immediate cause for canceling the interview. It doesn't matter that traffic backed up, your cat threw up a hairball, or you just got lost in the elevator. Being on time is not racing down the final corridor with moments to spare. Some interviewers agree with New York Giants football coach Tom Coughlin, who declared that team members were late for meetings if they didn't show up fifteen minutes early. Poor grooming is a basic turnoff. Wearing so much perfume or cologne that a gasping interviewer lunges for the window isn't recommended. Nor is wearing more makeup than a runway model, clanking along with a pocketful of change or an armload of bangles and bells, or sporting an unkempt beard (or, for some interviewers, even fashionable stubble).

Given the tube tops, sneakers, short skirts, and patterned stockings I've seen waltz through my door (and all on one candidate!), some of you may need to review the appropriate dress for every interview. While women no longer need to sport a black business suit and pearls, dressing tastefully in professional apparel is still a must. And that black suit will still work in most environments. Men should wear a white or light blue shirt, conservative suit, silk tie, and shined dress shoes. No one should think of wearing ties that glow in the dark, T-shirts advertising anything (but especially not X-rated), or any clothes even you know are totally unprofessional. Lies, damn lies, and statistics If you lie about anything—especially where and when you worked, what you did, where and when (or even if) you attended college— you will be caught. No matter how lowly the job, there are significant expenses involved with hiring someone to perform it. So companies will take the time to check out references. The higher up the food chain you climb, the more intense their scrutiny. Even if the lie is inconsequential, the very fact that you lied will, in virtually all instances, be immediate grounds for dismissal. Lacking a particular skill or experience may not automatically exclude you from getting the job. Lying about it will. Just ask former NBC news anchor Brian Williams about the consequences of "shading" the truth or "misremembering" an experience. While honesty may be the best (and only) policy, it is not necessary to share anything and everything with your interviewer. Anything you do in the privacy of your own home is not something you need to share. And do be smart enough, when asked what interests you about the job, not to answer, "Heck, I just need a job with benefits. I'm three months along and can't wait until my maternity leave starts."

The eyes have it Don't underestimate the effect of your own body language on the interviewer. While many people don't mean what they say or say what they mean, their nonverbal actions reveal exactly what they're feeling. According to studies, more than half of what we are trying to communicate is being received nonverbally. To many interviewers, your failure to "look them in the eye" indicates you have something to hide, as does being overly fidgety or nervous. Greet the interviewer with a firm handshake, face him or her, sit straight up, and, of course, look them in the eye. Breaking eye contact occasionally is also a good idea. Staring without pause for more than a few seconds will make almost anyone nervous. Likewise, interviewers are looking for people who are enthusiastic about what they do, so sighing, looking out the window, or checking your watch during a question will not create the right impression. If you don't seem interested in the job, why should they be interested in hiring you? But you can be too aggressive. One candidate said to me, barely five minutes into our interview, "I've got three other offers right now. What can you do for me?" I showed him where the exit was. Yes, you need to be confident, enthusiastic, and cheerful (and brave and clean and reverent...), but, as this example clearly illustrates, you can overplay your hand Avoid becoming defensive when there doesn't appear to be a reason: The interviewer asks what she thinks is a simple question and you act as if she has accused you of a crime. You start to sweat, hem and haw, and try to change the subject. What are you hiding? That's what the interviewer will be thinking. And if you aren't actually hiding anything, why are you acting so defensively? Try to make every minute of your interview a positive experience—introducing negativity of any kind is virtually guaranteed

to dim your chances. (Which is why the interviewer may introduce negativity, just to see how you handle it.) So complaining about your last job, boss, duties...or even the elevator ride upstairs...is getting yourself off on the wrong foot. ...And this is my mom There should be a new reality series featuring the bizarre behavior of some interviewees, as they chew, burp, scratch, swear, cry, laugh, and scream their way into our hearts. Interviewees have shown up drunk or stoned, brought their mothers with them, fallen asleep, even gone to the bathroom and never returned. Keeping your cell phone on during the interview qualifies as inappropriate behavior. Actually receiving or making a call ranks as bizarre. Remember what the interviewer is thinking: If this is your best behavior, what (gasp!) do I have to look forward to? Eat, drink, go home Interviewing over lunch is a situation fraught with potential dangers. Slurping spaghetti or soup or wiping barbeque sauce off your tie is simply not attractive, even if you are. Ordering the most (or least) expensive item on the menu sends an unwelcome message. And what happens when the French dish you didn't understand but ordered anyway turns out to be something you can't even look at, let alone eat? If you can't avoid a lunch interview (and I would certainly try), use your common sense. Order something light and reasonably priced—you're not really there for the food, are you? Remember what Mom told you—keep your elbows off the table, don't talk with your mouth full, and put your napkin in your lap. Don't drink alcohol (even wine), don't smoke (even if your host does), don't complain about the food (even if it was lousy), and don't forget that this is still an interview!

"And then I worked for…oops!" Throughout this book, I will attempt to give you the ability to formulate answers that respond to what the interviewer really wants to know. The more responsive your answer is to the interviewer's stated (or unstated) needs, the better. Since the best answers are "customized" to fit the company's needs and your qualifications, it's often difficult, if not impossible, to say that a particular answer is "right" or "wrong." But there are answers that are clearly wrong: Ö Any answer, no matter how articulate and specific, that fails to actually answer the question asked. Ö Any answer that reveals you are clearly unqualified for the job. Ö Any answer that provides information that doesn't jibe with your resume and/or cover letter. (Don't laugh. I, for one, have proudly given details about a job I left off my resume. The interviewer didn't laugh either.) Ö Any answer that reveals an inability to take responsibility for failures, weaknesses, poor decisions, and bad results or that tries to take full credit for a project to which others clearly contributed. Although many interviewers will not consider inappropriate dress, poor grooming, or a bit too much candor an automatic reason for dismissal, an accumulation of two or more such actions may force even the most empathetic to question your suitability. (Some items, of course, such as dishonesty, may well lead to an immediate and heartfelt, "Thank you…please leave.") Do your best Sherlock Holmes You also need to always gauge the interviewer's response to what you're saying, not just the answers you've given but the questions you've asked. Listen for verbal clues and watch the body language.

that will often tell you how you're really doing. Again, you don't want to kill a potential job because you were overly aggressive on the interview. If you know what to look for, you'll get extra clues from the body language of an interviewer: Lack of eye contact or "shifting" eyes are usually seen as a sign of dishonesty or, at best, discomfort: "Mr. Interviewer, are you planning any more layoffs?" {squint, shift, squirm, blink…) "Uh, no, Jim. So, how about dem Bears?" Raised eyebrows indicate disbelief or even mild distain, along the lines of "Oh, really?"/"You don't mean that, do you?"/"Gee, how'd you figure that out?"/"You don't actually expect me to buy that, do you?" A smile at the wrong time can be a sign of discomfort or an indication of a complete lack of appropriate social skills. A tightly clenched jaw, pursed lips, or a forced smile may indicate stress, anything from a boss's reprimand to an early morning fight with a spouse. While the cause is clearly not your problem, you need to make sure the effect does not become a distraction during your interview. "Closed" positions of the hands and arms—clenched fists, arms folded across the body—are not positive. They may also indicate boredom or negativity. An interviewer who is slumping or leaning back in his chair may be showing disrespect, arrogance, or disinterest. It is surely a sign that you have to ask a question to get him back into the conversation. If the interviewer keeps nodding rapidly for an extended period of time while you are asking or answering a question, it may be shorthand for "Be quiet and let me say something now." Doodling, chewing on a pencil, scratching, playing with one's hands, moving things around on a desk, or acting distracted are typical signs of nervousness. Don't interpret it as anything more than nerves unless something else tips you off. Again, ask a question to get the focus back on you or, even better, a question about her. Most people like to talk about themselves, especially a not-too-experienced interviewer who seems to be nervous about interviewing you, believe it or not! But don't overanalyze the situation. An interviewer vigorously rubbing her eyes may just be telling you she didn't get enough sleep last night or is suffering from allergies. Let's get ready to rumble Most job candidates think of the interview in completely the wrong way—as an interrogation or police lineup. And they see themselves as suspects, not as the key prospects they really are. This book will show you that you are, to a very large degree, in charge of the interview. It will convince you that you are there not only to sell the company on you, but to make sure that you are sold on them. It will give you the powerful questions that will work whatever your age, whatever your experience, whatever your goals. Despite my sterling reputation with employment offices, the first edition of this book became a bestseller. In fact, it continues to sell, year after year. I don't pretend to know why it has done as well as it has, but I will hazard a guess: It is simple, straightforward, practical, and written in a welcoming and humorous style. (Okay, I suppose that counts as four and a half guesses.) And it has clearly helped literally hundreds of thousands of candidates prepare for every type of interview and every style of interviewer. I'm pleased and proud that this new edition will help many more of you! It will not, however, spend very much time preparing you for the questions you need to ask during the interview. Luckily for you, I've already written the companion book to this one—101 Smart Questions to Ask on Your Interview—whose sole purpose is to do exactly that. And I have just revised it as well. Using these two books together, you will be amply armed for any interview and any interviewer.

2

The Interview Process

You'll probably have to go through more interviews than your predecessors for the same job, no matter what your level of expertise. Knowledge and experience still give you an inside edge. But these days, you'll need stamina, too. Your honesty, your intelligence, your mental health—even the toxicity of your blood—may be measured before you can be considered fully assessed. You may also have to tiptoe through a minefield of different types of interview situations. Do all you can to remain confident and flexible and ready with your answers. No matter what kind of interview you find yourself facing, this approach should carry you through with flying colors. Let's take a brief tour of the interview circuit. Is this the person to whom I am speaking? Telephone screening is an effective tactic used by many interviewers, but some rely on the strategy as a primary means of qualifying candidates. For many of these interviewers, the in-person interview is little more than an opportunity to confirm what they feel they've already learned on the phone. Interviewers who typically fall into this category are entrepreneurs, CEOs, high-level executives, and others short on time and long on vision. Their guiding philosophy could be summed up as: "I have a personnel problem to solve, and I don't plan to waste my valuable time talking in person to anybody but the very best." A telephone screener is also often the dominant interviewer at small- to mid-size companies where no formal Human Resources (or Personnel) department exists or where such a department has only recently been created. The primary objective of the telephone screener is to identify reasons to remove you from active consideration before scheduling an in-person meeting. Among the common reasons for abrupt removal from the telephone screener's short list: evidence that there's a disparity between your resume and actual experience, poor verbal communication skills, lack of required technical skills. If you are expecting a call (or calls) from telephone screeners, make sure family members know how to answer the phone. Hint: A sullen "Huh?" from your teenage son or brother is not the best way. And by all means avoid cutesy answering machine tapes: "Hi!" [giggle, giggle] "We're upstairs getting nasty!" [giggle, snort] "So leave a message, dude." What could be better than answering questions from the comfort of your own home? For starters, conducting a telephone interview has cost you two valuable tools you can employ during in-person interviews: eye contact and body language. You're left with your skills, the facts on your resume, and your ability to communicate verbally. Don't be discouraged. Always project a positive image through your voice and your answers. Don't overdo it, but don't let the telephone be your undoing either. If your confidence is flagging, try smiling while you listen and speak. Sure, it might look silly— but it absolutely changes the tone and timbre of one's voice. I also like to stand, even walk around, during a telephone interview. It seems to simultaneously calm me down and give me more energy. You have a right to be prepared for any interview. Chances are the interviewer will call you to set a time for the telephone interview. However, if she fires a question at you as soon as you answer the phone, there's nothing wrong with asking her to call back at a mutually agreeable time. You need to prepare your surroundings for a successful interview. Next to the phone, you'll want to have a copy of your resume (which you've quickly reviewed), the cover letter you sent or emailed, a list of questions you've prepared for them, a notepad, your research materials on that company, and a glass of water. You will also want to have already answered nature's call—you surely don't want to excuse yourself in the middle of the interview—and placed a "Do Not Disturb" sign on your door, so family members or roommates don't interrupt. You never want to put the interviewer on hold for any reason. Are you wheat or chaff? Many personnel professionals fall into a different category: human screens. For them, interviewing is not simply a once-aquarter or once-a-month event, but rather a key part of their daily job descriptions. They meet and interview many people, and are more likely than a telephone screener to consider an exceptional applicant for more than one opening within the organization. A primary objective of a human screen is to develop a strong group of candidates for managers (the third kind of interviewer) to interview in person. To do this, of course, they must fend off many applicants and callers—a daunting task, because the human screen or the department in which he works is often the only contact provided in employment listings or posts. Among the most common reasons for removal from a human screen's "hot" list are: lack of the formal or informal qualifications outlined in the organization's job description; sudden changes in hiring priorities and/or personnel requirements; poor performance during the in-person interview itself; and inaction due to uncertainty about your current status or contact information. That last reason is more common than you might imagine. Human screens are usually swamped with phone calls, emails, texts, resumes, and unannounced visits from hopeful applicants. Despite their best efforts, they sometimes lose track of qualified people. Human screens excel at separating the wheat from the chaff. Because they are exposed to a wide variety of candidates on a regular basis, they usually boast more face-to-face interviewing experience than members of the other two groups. They may be more likely to spot inconsistencies or outright lies on resumes, simply because they've seen so many over the years that they know when a candidate's credentials for a given position don't quite pass the "smell test." And while interviews with a telephone screener or the hiring manager may be rushed because of their hectic schedules, human screens are often able to spend a comparatively long amount of time with particularly qualified candidates. Not surprisingly, human screens often react with a puzzled look if others ask them to offer their "gut reaction" to a particular candidate. Because they're generally operating a step removed from the work itself, their assessments of candidates may be more black and white than gray: Either the candidate has three years of appropriate experience or she doesn't. Either he has been trained in computer design or he hasn't. Of course, this analysis may overlook important interpersonal issues. Why you should avoid Human Resources There aren't many career books that will advise you to make a beeline for the Human Resources department of a company you've targeted. In fact, most, if not all, will tell you to avoid it like the plague if at all possible. What have these poor (formerly personnel) people done to generate such animosity? Nothing at all. I'm sure many of them are very nice people who do their jobs very well. The problem is that their jobs have little to do with actually getting you a job. They are not seeking candidates to interview and hire; they are trying to maximize the number they can eliminate. They can say no. And they do. A lot. But they can't say yes.

In addition to not being able to actually offer you anything more than coffee or tea (and maybe a personality or drug test), many Human Resources departments may have (surprisingly) little idea about what hiring managers really want in job applicants. The more technical or specialized the field, the truer this statement. I know of a Human Resources director who recommended a candidate for whom English was a second—and not very good— language for the top editorial post on a major association magazine. Another passed along a candidate who scored 55 (out of 100) on a spelling test for a proofreading position. Still another recommended someone whose resume was filled with rather obvious or easily discovered lies for a vice president of finance position. At many organizations, even hiring managers make it a point to bypass their Human Resources departments—bringing candidates in, interviewing them, and only then passing them along so Human Resources can take care of the paperwork. Make it easier for the hiring manager to do just that. Make every effort to get in touch with him or her directly, preferably by dropping the name of a "friend of a friend." If you have to go through Human Resources (and sometimes despite your best efforts you will), you can't ignore their power: They're the only ones who can get you to the next level—the real interview. So it certainly would be sensible to make friends with them and use them in whatever way you can. Nevertheless, you will probably not go wrong if you presume that the Human Resources person conducting a screening interview has no time to become your best friend, knows little or nothing about the job you so desperately want, and knows even less about the hiring manager. Meet your new boss The hiring manager may not be the person for whom you will be working, but probably will be. Even where others have strong input, most companies still allow managers to hire their own staff, within certain parameters. He is probably a supervisor who has chosen (or is required) to shoehorn in-person interviews into his busy workdays. (In smaller companies especially, the president may be the ultimate decision maker, even if you won't be reporting to her.) A manager who has worked with a number of previous employees who held the same position will bring a unique perspective to the proceedings. What's different about interviewing with the hiring manager as opposed to your time with a recruiter or headhunter or even Human Resources? This is the person you actually have to impress, the only one who can say those magic words, "You're hired. When can you start?" The hiring manager's primary objective is to evaluate your skills and measure your personal chemistry on a firsthand basis. These interviewers want to get to know everything they can about the people with whom they'll be working closely. (As we've seen, the telephone screener may well be an entrepreneur who delegates heavily and interacts only intermittently with new hires. And the human screen usually has nothing to do with the day-today operation of the company.) Common reasons for being dropped from a hiring manager's hot list include: lack of personal chemistry or rapport; poor performance during the interview itself; and her assessment that, although you're qualified and personable, you would simply not fit in well with the team. Many hiring managers have a highly intuitive sense of who will (and won't) perform the job well and achieve a good "fit" with the rest of the work group. On the other hand, it sometimes comes as a surprise to applicants that excellent supervisors can be less than stellar interviewers. But a great many managers lack any formal training in the art of interviewing. Of the three categories of interviewers, this is the group most likely to interpret the interview as an opportunity to "get to know" more about you, rather than require specific answers to questions about your background, experience, outlook on work, and interpersonal skills. The hiring interview Your first interview with the person who will manage your prospective position is not likely to be a walk in the park. You may be stepping out of the range of the experience and interviewing talent of the Human Resources professional and into unknown territory. And you could wander there for a while. Why? Experienced interviewers are trained to stay in charge of the interview, not let it meander down some dead-end, nonproductive track. There is a level of predictability to the way they conduct interviews, even if they utilize different techniques. On the other hand, the hiring manager is sure to lack some or all of the screening interviewer's knowledge, experience, and skill, making him an unpredictable animal. Foiling the inept interviewer A majority of corporate managers don't know what it takes to hire the right candidate. Few of them have had formal training in conducting interviews of any kind. To make things worse, most managers feel slightly less comfortable conducting the interview than the nervous candidate sitting across their desks from them! A manager might decide you are not the right person for the job, without ever realizing that the questions he asked were so ambiguous, so off the mark, that even the perfect candidate could not have stumbled on the "right" answers. No one monitors the performance of the interviewer. And the candidate cannot be a mind reader. So more often than is necessary, otherwise perfectly qualified candidates walk out the door for good...simply because the manager failed at the interview! But that doesn't have to happen to you. You can—and should—be prepared to put your best foot forward, no matter what the experience or expertise of the manager interviewing you. You'll be a step ahead of the game (and the other candidates) if you realize at the outset that the interviewer is after more than just facts about your skills and background. He is waiting for something more elusive to hit him, something he may not even be able to articulate: He wants to feel that, somehow, you "fit" the organization or department. Knowing what you're up against is half the battle. Rather than sit back passively and hope for the best, you can help the unskilled interviewer focus on how your unique skills can directly benefit— fit—the department or organization by citing a number of specific examples. What other unusual problems could you face during an interview? Yada, yada, yada Dwayne thinks he's a pretty good interviewer. He has a list of 15 questions he asks every candidate—same questions, same order, every time. He takes notes on their answers and asks an occasional follow-up question. He gives them a chance to ask questions. He's friendly, humorous, and excited about working at Netcorp.com...as he tells every candidate...in detail...for hours. Then he wonders why so many candidates decline additional interviews and only a small fraction of his hires pan out. I've never really understood the interviewer who thinks telling the story of his or her life is pertinent. Why do some interviewers do it? Partly nervousness, partly inexperience, but mostly because they have the mistaken notion they have to sell you on the company, rather than the other way around. There are occasions when this may be necessary—periods of low unemployment, a glut of particular jobs and a dearth of qualified candidates, a candidate who's so desirable the interviewer feels, perhaps correctly, that he or she has to outsell and outbid the competition.

Under most circumstances, you should be expected to carry the conversational load, while the interviewer sits back and decides if he or she is ready to buy what you're selling. Is it to your benefit to find yourself seated before Mr. Monologue? You might think so. After all, while he's waxing poetic about the new cafeteria, you don't have to worry about inserting your other foot in your mouth. No explaining that last firing or why you've had four jobs in three months. Nope, just sit back, relax, and try to stay awake. But I don't believe Mr. M. is doing you any favors. Someone who monopolizes the conversation doesn't give you the opportunity you need to "strut your stuff." You may want to avoid leaving a bad impression, but I doubt you want to leave no impression at all. As long as you follow the advice in this book and, especially, this chapter, you should welcome the savvy interviewer who asks the open-ended, probing questions he needs to identify the right person for the job—the same questions you need to convince him it's you. Let's all get stoned Yes, interviewers have been known to be drunk, stoned, or otherwise incapacitated. Some have spent virtually the entire time allotted to a candidate speaking on the phone or browsing email. Others have gone off on tirades about interoffice disputes or turf wars. If the interviewer treats you with such apparent indifference or disrespect before you're even hired, how do you expect him to act once you are hired? There is a boss out there willing to treat you with the same respect she would expect from you—it's just not this one. Move on. Approach and be seated There are a number of styles and guiding philosophies when it comes to person-to-person interviews. The overall purpose, of course, is to screen you out if you lack the aptitudes (and attitudes) the company is looking for.

Although experienced interviewers may use more than one strategy, it's essential to know which mode you're in at any given point—and what to do about it. Here's a summary of the methods and objectives of the most common approaches. The behavioral interview Your conversations with the interviewer will focus almost exclusively on your past experience as he tries to learn more about how you have already behaved in a variety of on-the-job situations. Then he will use this information to extrapolate your future reactions on the job. How did you handle yourself in some really tight spots? What kinds of on-the-job disasters have you survived? Did you do the right thing? What were the repercussions of your decisions? Be careful what you say. Every situation you faced was unique in its own way, so be sure the interviewer understands the specific limitations you had to deal with. Did you lack adequate staff? Support from management? Up-to-date software? If you made the mistake of plunging in too quickly, say so and admit that you've learned to think things through. Explain what you'd do differently the next time around. Remember: Those interviewers using a behavioral interview are trying to ensure you can really walk the walk, not just talk the talk. So leave out the generalizations and philosophizing and don't get lost in the details. In other words, just tell them the problem you faced, the action you took, and the results you achieved, without exaggeration. Which is why composing three, four, or more "stories"— actual experiences that illustrate your most important skills or qualifications—is important. Just make sure to structure them in "Problem-Solution-Action" format. The competency-based interview You will know you are facing a competency-based interview by the way the questions are structured. Instead of open-ended questions, which give you virtually carte blanche to choose examples and target your answer the way you want to, you will face more specific questions, such as: Tell me about the last time you missed a deadline. Tell me about your most recent project that included a forensic audit. Describe what you did the last time your boss rejected one of your ideas. Give me a recent example of how you led a team to successfully complete a challenging task. Describe a situation where you had to deal with a difficult client (customer, employee, team member). How did you diffuse the situation? Such questions are designed to measure your level of individual responsibility, decisiveness, independence, ambition, and initiative; analytical skills; "people" skills; and management and leadership skills, including your ability to plan, strategize, motivate, implement, and delegate. Specific industries, companies, or departments will require specific skills or competencies, what they consider the key characteristics it takes to be successful in a particular position. A bank's required competencies may range from auditing to securities law, from credit analysis to risk management. A large manufacturer may desire someone with skills in cost containment, inventory control, production processes, safety training, or other such areas. A well-prepared interviewer will have a list of questions designed to elicit specific and detailed examples to prove you can do exactly what her company requires. And you should have identified the particular skills and abilities—your competencies—you know are required and have examples at the ready. If you lack a particular attribute, be prepared to explain why you are unable to cite a specific example that touts that competency. (If you had been properly screened, of course, your lack of such a competency would have eliminated you from consideration right from the start.) There is more information on how to handle competencybased questions in Chapter 6. For an even more detailed explanation of how to prepare for this kind of interview, I suggest Robin Kessler's book, Competency-based Interviews. The team interview Today's organizational hierarchies are becoming flatter. That means that people at every level of a company are more likely to become involved in a variety of projects and tasks, including interviewing you. The team interview can range from a pleasant conversation to a torturous interrogation. Typically, you will meet with a group, or "team," of interviewers around a table in a conference room. They may be members of your prospective department or a cross section of employees from throughout the company. (A slightly less stressful variation is the "tag team" approach, in which a single questioner exits and is followed by a different questioner a few minutes [or questions] later.) Rarely will you be informed beforehand to expect a team interview. The hiring manager or someone from Human Resources may chair an orderly session of question-and-answer—or turn the group loose to shoot questions at you like a firing squad. When it's all over, you'll have to survive the assessment of every member of the group. Some hiring managers will consult with the group after the interview for an evaluation of your performance. Others determine their decision using group consensus. The good news is that you don't have to worry that the subjective opinion of just one person will determine your shot at the job. If one member of the group thinks you lacked confidence or came across as arrogant, others in the group may disagree. The interviewer who leveled the criticism will have to defend her opinion to the satisfaction of the group—or be shot down herself.A group of people is also more likely (but not guaranteed) to ask you a broader range of questions that may uncover and underline your skills and expertise. Just take your time and treat every member of the team with the same respect and deference you would the hiring manager. If you face a series of separate interrogations with a variety of interviewers and are asked many of the same questions, be sure to vary your answers. Cite different projects, experiences, successes, even failures. Otherwise, when they meet to compare notes, you'll come off as a "Johnny One Note." The case (situational, hypothetical) interview Our salespeople haven't met quota for the last three quarters. We overcharged one of our biggest customers, who is now threatening to give all her business to our biggest competitor. You caught your boss grossly padding his expense account. What would you do? Hypothetical ("what if...?") questions are the basis of a case or situational interview, in which the interviewer conjures up a series of situations, real or imaginary, in order to ascertain whether you have the resourcefulness, logic, creativity, and ability to think under pressure. Why apply such pressure? Even the best-prepared candidates can't prepare for these questions! If you are seeking a position at a consulting company, law firm or a counseling organization, you should expect to confront this type of interview. What most interviewers want to see is a combination of real-world experience, inspired creativity, and the willingness to acknowledge when more information or assistance is in order. (Many interviewers will pose hypothetical questions designed to smoke out people who find it difficult to reach out to other team members for help.) They want to understand how you approach a problem, the framework within which you seek a solution, and the thought process you utilize. Situational interview questions can come in any shape or style. If you have a detailed description of the job you're applying for, use your imagination to try to anticipate a number of situations that might come up. You will have to devote a great deal of thought to each of these questions. If you find yourself caught in this snare, stay calm and use the homework you have done on your personal inventory to untangle yourself. Here are some tips for confronting a case interview: Ö Admit that a tough situation would make you nervous. You might even panic momentarily. No interviewer is looking for a candidate bent on plunging right in, then flailing about without considering consequences or alternatives. Nervousness begets the adrenaline that often fuels creative strategies. Ö Take a moment to think before you answer. This shows you are not likely to plunge into any situation with a hotheaded response. Rather, you are taking the time to weigh the alternatives and choose the best course of action. The more complicated the problem, the more time you're expected to take. Ö Take notes on the problem that's presented. Ask questions about the details. Be aware that not all information is pertinent to the solution. (That wily interviewer!) Ö Avoid generalizations. The interviewer will want to hear concrete steps that will lead to a solution, not your philosophy of how to approach the problem. Ö Don't get lost in the details. The interviewer wants to see how you approach the broad problem, so set your sights on the most important factors.

Ö Ask questions. Ö Share your thoughts—out loud. That's really what the interviewer wants to hear. Ö There's nothing wrong with a creative approach, but it should always be set within a logical framework. No matter what the interview technique, quash the temptation to exaggerate or downright fabricate a response. Ö Plan your answers to a number of different situations ahead of time. Assume that some of these questions will be about areas of knowledge and skill you have yet to develop, so learn as much as you can about what you don't know. And have a strategy for finding the information or resources you currently lack. Ö Ask questions! While case interviews are geared to upper-echelon candidates, candidates for many different kinds of jobs may be given the opportunity to walk the walk—to show what they can actually do on the job: Clerks may be given typing or filing tests; copy editors given minutes to edit a magazine article or book chapter; a salesperson may be asked to telephone and sell a prospect; and a computer programmer may be required to create some code. The more technical the job, the more likely an interviewer will not simply "take you at your word" that you are capable of doing it. The stress interview

Formal qualifications are important, but in some jobs, the emotional demands, sudden emergencies, and breakneck pace of work can be downright intimidating—not once in a while, but every day. Even a candidate who knows all the technical moves may wilt under the glare of an etiquette-challenged boss or crumble when inheriting a surrealistically compressed deadline. When you're interviewing for such a position—whether you're seeking a job as a commodities trader, air traffic controller, or prison guard—an interviewer may feel it's almost meaningless to determine if you are capable of performing the job under the best conditions. He may well try to assess how you will do under the very worst conditions. And that's where the stress interview comes in. Anyone who's been through one of these never forgets it. A common enough question in this setting could sound gruff or rude, which is exactly how it's supposed to sound. Rather than a pleasant, "So, tell me about yourself," a stress interviewer may snarl (literally), "So, why the hell should I hire you for anything?" It's possible that the company is using this type of interview as a "covert" personality test. It may even be conducted by a psychologist or other professional who is trying to get you angry. Here are some techniques an interviewer may use: Ö He ridicules everything you say and questions why you're even interviewing at his company. Ö He says nothing when you walk into the room...and for five minutes afterward...then just stares at you after you answer his first question. Ö She keeps you waiting past the scheduled time and then keeps looking at her watch as you answer questions. Ö She stares out the window and seems to be completely uninterested in everything you have to say. Ö He challenges every answer, disagrees with every opinion, and interrupts you at every turn. Ö He doesn't introduce himself when you walk in, just hits you with a tough question. Ö She takes phone calls, works on her computer, and/ or eats lunch as you interview. Ö You may be seated in a broken chair, directly in front of a high-speed fan, or next to an open window...in the dead of winter.

How do you deal with this kind of manufactured stress? Ö Never let them see you sweat. No matter how stressful the situation, stay calm. When the interviewer finishes asking a question, take a few seconds to compose yourself and then, and only then, answer. Ö Recognize the situation for what it is. It's nothing more than an artificial scenario designed to see how you react under pressure. The interviewer (probably) has nothing against you personally. It's just a game, though not a pleasant one for you. Ö Don't become despondent. It's easy to think that the interviewer has taken a strong dislike to you and that your chances for completing the interview process are nil. That's not the case. The stress interview is designed to see if you will become depressed, hostile, or flustered when the going gets tough. Ö Watch your tone of voice. It's easy to become sarcastic during a stress interview, especially if you don't realize what the interviewer is up to. If you are subjected to a stress interview, you may well question seeking a job with a company that utilizes such techniques. If they think insulting and belittling you during the interview is acceptable, what's their management philosophy–gruel at nine, thumbscrews at two? Don't confuse a stress interview with a negative interview. In the latter, the interviewer merely highlights the (supposedly) negative aspects of the job at every opportunity. He may even make some up: "Would you have any problem cleaning the toilets every Saturday morning?" or "Is three hours of daily overtime a problem for you?" The brainteaser interview Microsoft interviewers have famously been known to ask, "How would you move Mount Fuji?" The list of questions designed to assess how creatively you approach a problem—as opposed to the logical approach case interviews are designed to highlight—are virtually unlimited: Ö How many people still smoke in Finland? Ö How many people surf in California at least once a month? Ö How many acres of ranchland are there in Mexico? Ö How many accountants are there in New York State? Ö How would you build a better mousetrap? Most of the same tips I gave you when approaching a case interview are still pertinent—take your time, ask pertinent questions, then talk through the approach you would take to answer the question. Make whatever statistical assumptions you need to make—the interviewer doesn't care if you know the population of Finland, just how you would come up with an answer (which may have no relation to reality). She may not have any idea of the "correct" answer to such a question herself. Don't wear flip flops at a buttoned-down firm Birds of a feather do flock together. And different companies tend to attract particular "species" of employees. A company's physical environment, management attitude and policies, and the personality of the "birds" that predominate comprise its corporate culture. Is it a "loose" atmosphere with jean-clad creative types running amok? Or a buttoned-down, blue-suited autocracy with a long list of rules to follow during timed coffee breaks? Some companies are dominated by a single personality— a still-active founder or an executive who has exerted a strong, long-lasting influence on policies and style. Think Steve Jobs at Apple, Bill Gates at Microsoft, or Larry Ellison at Oracle. While there are exceptions, such companies tend to be "closely held" fiefdoms whose every level reflects the "cult of personality." If that personality is a despot, benign or otherwise, even a decentralized management structure won't create a company everyone wants to work for. Family-owned companies often pose similar problems. Your chances to make decisions and take responsibility may be tied to your last name. Barely competent family members may wind up with cushy jobs and high pay, while you and other "outsiders" do all the work. While many such firms are privately held, even publicly traded companies in which family members hold a significant block of stock (like Ford, Walton, or DuPont) may sometimes err on the side of nepotism. Many larger, more decentralized companies will spread decision-making power and opportunities for advancement somewhat more evenly. However, such companies often encourage competition among workers rather than focusing their collective energies on competing organizations. If managers regularly spend half their time politicking or writing self-serving memos to the boss, it's a survival-of-the-fittest (or survival-of-the-best-memo-writer) atmosphere. People attuned to corporate infighting might relish such a company; those who just want to do their jobs and be rewarded for the work they do will find it an unfriendly place to work. Some companies are bursting with energy; their offices reverberate with a steady hum of activity. Such a high-key environment is right for aggressive go-getters who are unafraid of such a fast pace and more than ready, even eager, to jump into the fray. Other workplaces are calmer, quiet, almost studious in nature. Such low-key firms are probably better choices for those of you with more laid-back personalities. While a high-energy or low-key atmosphere says little about a particular company's chances for success, it may have a lot to do with your own on-the-job performance, success, and happiness. Matching dissimilar corporate and individual personalities usually results in a new job search. If you run across a company that seems to give off no signals at all, beware! This is usually the directionless organization, one that lacks both an agenda and dynamic leadership. Without such leadership, you can be certain that this organization will founder, usually when things start going wrong and the timely implementation of company-wide decisions is required. The more you know about the companies you're considering, the better off you'll be. Don't believe everything you read And don't believe everything company representatives tell you. Just as employees have been known to "forget" a job when writing their resume and slightly exaggerate their responsibilities at others, employers have been known to tell attractive candidates what they want to hear. Except, unfortunately, for the one Neanderthal who just happens to be...your prospective boss. Companies sometimes consciously misstate job requirements so as to attract, they believe, the "higher end" of the applicant pool. If their gut feeling is that the job requires two years of experience, they may say three are required, expecting a higher grade of queries. They may also believe that the few people who do contact them with only two years of experience will likely be more motivated than the average applicant. This is called an "enhanced excluder," a means of setting the bar slightly higher than they need to, knowing they can always ignore the standards they've set for the right candidate. Some companies use this method almost as a pre-interviewing technique, a way to see which applicants try to get around the announced requirements...and how compelling a case they can make for themselves. If candidates absolutely, positively, have to have particular technical expertise, that requirement should be prominently, specifically, and emphatically featured in the job posting. This sounds self-evident, but you'd be surprised at the number of hiring managers I've spoken to who don't specify particular skills they're seeking...and then complain about the experience levels of the candidates they interview. Ambiguous requirements like "good computer skills" will never help an employer attract the skilled people it is seeking. And they certainly won't help you figure out whether you're qualified for the position! Are you overqualified? This, of course, is a question you really should ask yourself before you go on any interview. It's essential to admit—at least to yourself—if you are seriously overqualified for a position. Many of you might think it's easier to get a job beneath your qualifications—to work as an accounting assistant when you've been a full-charge bookkeeper, to be a receptionist when you've been an office manager, to go back to sales after rising to sales manager. It isn't. You may have more qualifications than the job requires, but you may no longer have the specific qualifications it demands. While you may have overseen a 20-person sales force and be known far and wide as an ace motivator, you will have trouble getting a job selling copy machines. Why? Because they don't care about your management and motivational credentials. Nor do they need them. They want to know how many copy machines you're capable of selling a month. And they do care that you've never sold one! Employers may question the motivation of someone willing to "do almost anything." Will such an employee just show up, do what's asked but nothing more? What about someone willing to work "for almost nothing"? To quote another cliché: You get what you pay for. And that's exactly what "almost nothing" is worth. Especially in lower-level jobs, employers want people happy to be doing what they were hired to do, not constantly pointing out that they could do the boss's job better than he could. The office manager wants to treat the receptionist as a receptionist, not someone who has been an office manager and may, indeed, know more than he does about running an office. Just as some managers worry about hiring underlings who they fear may one day outshine them, many people worry about hiring people for low-level jobs who have already done what their boss is doing. It's disconcerting and, to many, highly threatening. Is it okay to take notes? Since it is okay for the interviewer to take notes, I believe it is fine, even encouraged, for you to do so. Why? There are a few good reasons: You should walk in with notes—the questions you intend to ask, specific points you want to remember, research data you want to incorporate in an answer or question. Getting the interviewer used to your "consulting my notes" makes it a lot easier to ask permission to take notes during the interview itself. But be careful. You don't want to appear to be constantly referring to your notes every time the interviewer asks a question: "Where did you go to college, Jim?" "Uh, just a minute, let me consult my notes." You can't possibly remember everything...no matter how good your memory. And yet you certainly want to remember what you said, what he said, what seemed right, what felt wrong, titles, numbers...all the myriad things that went on during the interview. As long as you ask permission first, I believe taking notes is an absolute requirement. Third, it is essential for your follow-up. I encourage you to write brief individual notes or emails to every person you meet on an interview, from the receptionist to the person who got your coffee, and even more targeted and longer letters or emails to all the people with whom you actually interviewed. How can you be sure of the correct spelling of that many names, titles, and so on without good notes? How can you make sure to answer (again) the objection you know may be the key thing obstructing your hiring? How can you schmooze the colleague who seemed a little cold to your candidacy, perhaps jealous because she wanted (or expected) your job?

And last, you may need to use your notes in the interview itself—jotting down a question you don't want to forget (while the interviewer drones on), a point you want to raise, an example you want to emphasize. This will allow you to bring up a point when it's the right time, which may be quite awhile down the road, even at the very end of the interview. Personally, I wouldn't want anything but an attractive notebook that is extracted from an equally professional looking briefcase, along with a quality pen (not a disposable). Most recent graduates might be more comfortable toting an iPad or other tablet, which I think most interviewers would now find acceptable. Many if not most interviewers will interpret your note taking as a sign of professionalism and seriousness, as long as you don't keep your nose buried in your notebook or iPad the entire time. Whatever you use, remember, the point of the interview is to listen, then talk. Write as little as you need. And if you aren't very good at note taking and listening at the same time (or taking notes while retaining eye contact), practice. No one wants to talk to your forehead. Don't run away...yet We've all been there—an interview that is obviously not working. Maybe it's the interviewer, maybe it's you, maybe it's the weather, maybe it's a cruel joke by the universe. In any event, the interview is clearly not going well and you are sorely tempted to get up, thank the interviewer, and run, not walk, to the safety of your bedroom. Fight the impulse to flee. Excuse yourself, perhaps for a bathroom break. (Hey, I know it's not usually done, but right now we're trying to salvage an interview that's going down in flames.) Compose yourself. Give yourself a pep talk. Then go back in there and sell yourself.

How to "Ace" Any Interview Relax! Think of it as an adventure (as opposed to a tribunal). Try to enjoy yourself. Imagine that the interviewer is a sports star, famous author, or movie celebrity you've always admired. Keep smiling. No, not a fake grin, just maintain a pleasant, relaxed smile that is, hopefully, a by-product of your involvement in an interesting conversation. Put yourself in the interviewer's place. Wouldn't you want to work with such an agreeable person? Be enthusiastic. About the position, your accomplishments, and what you know about the company. But don't gush—if you're not genuinely enthusiastic, you'll come across as a phony. Be honest. Lying about even the smallest or least important details could be grounds for immediate departure. Make lots of eye contact. Have you ever known someone who wouldn't look you in the eye? After a while, you probably started to wonder what that person had to hide. You don't want your interviewer wondering anything of the sort. So meet his or her eyes while you're shaking hands, then frequently throughout the interview. But don't stare—unrelenting eye contact is worse than none at all. Stay positive. As we'll see when we discuss questions about your previous jobs, you must learn to put a positive spin on everything, but especially loaded issues, such as your reason for leaving a job, troubled relations with your superiors, or the lack of required qualifications. Don't let an unskilled interviewer trip you up. Make sure the preparation you've spent so much time on comes shining through, especially when a manager throws you a curve. If need be, your advance preparation should give you the power to take control of the interview, allowing you to emphasize the many ways in which you will benefit the prospective employer.

You may actually be completely wrong for the job, which is why the interview is not going well. But that doesn't mean there aren't other jobs at that company or jobs at other companies the interviewer knows. So hang in there a little longer. And if you are rejected despite your best efforts, you may learn something—especially if you ask—that will improve your interviewing skills or performance. Should you reject an actual offer out of hand because you've decided the job, company, or boss is completely wrong? I wouldn't. Take at least a night to think about any offer away from the stresses of the interview process. Your thinking may change.

3

Who Are You?

The success or failure of many interviews will hinge on your ability to clearly define who you are, what you know, and what you can do. The interviewing process is a kind of sale. In this case, you are the product—and the salesperson. If you show up unprepared to talk about your unique features and benefits, you're not likely to motivate an interviewer to "buy." The sad fact is that many job candidates are unprepared to talk about themselves. You may have produced a gorgeous resume and cover letter. You may be wearing the perfect clothes on the day of the interview. But if you can't convince the interviewer—face to face—that you are the right person for the job, you aren't likely to make the sale. Too many candidates hesitate after the first open-ended question, then stumble and stutter their way through a disjointed litany of resume "sound bites." Other interviewees recite canned replies that only highlight their memory skills. I am assuming that, like most people, you are a complex product made up of a unique blend of abilities, skills, and personal qualities and shaped by your own personal and professional history. Believe me, the time you spend outlining the details of your own life will pay off in interviews, and, ultimately, job offers. This chapter will guide you through the process.

What you should know about you

There are two steps you need to undertake. The first is to imitate the FBI and build a complete "dossier," a factual record of everything you have done and accomplished in your life and career. Your work experience Start by preparing a separate sheet of paper or file for every full-time and part-time job you have ever held, no matter how short the tenure. (Yes, even summer jobs are important here. They demonstrate resourcefulness, responsibility, and initiative— that you were already developing a sense of independence while you were still living at home.) Whether you choose to include some, all, or none of these short-term jobs on your resume or to discuss them during your interview is a decision you will make later. For now, write down everything about every job. For each employer, include: Ö Name, address, telephone number, and email address. Ö The names of all of your supervisors and, whenever possible, where they can be reached. Ö Letters of recommendation (especially if they can't be reached). Ö The exact dates (month and year) you were employed. For each job, include: Ö Specific duties and responsibilities. Ö Supervisory experience, noting the number of people you managed. Ö Specific skills required for the job. Ö Key accomplishments. Ö Dates you received promotions. Ö Any awards, honors, or special recognition you received. For each part-time job, also include the number of hours you worked per week.

You don't need to write a book on each job, but do provide specific data (volume of work handled, problems solved, dollars saved) to paint a detailed picture of your abilities and accomplishments. These hard facts will add a powerful punch to your interview presentation. Volunteer and internship experience Whether you were paid as a volunteer or intern is unimportant. What is important is what you learned and accomplished in any such position. So, again, create a detailed record of your volunteer pursuits or internships, similar to those you just completed for each job you held. For each company or organization for which you volunteered or interned, include: Ö Name, address, telephone number, and email address. Ö Name of your supervisor or the director of the organization. Ö Letter(s) of recommendation. Ö Exact dates (month and year) of your involvement with the organization. For each volunteer experience or internship, include: Ö Approximate number of hours devoted to the activity each month. Ö Specific duties and responsibilities. Ö Skills required. Ö Major accomplishments. Ö Awards, honors, or special recognition you received. Your educational achievements For each school you have attended, whatever its level, include its name, address, and phone number; years attended; major area of study; important (relevant) courses; honors; and GPA and/or class rank if pertinent or available. Which courses did you enjoy most? Which least? Which were your strongest subjects? Which were your weakest?

If you're a recent college graduate or are still in college, you don't need to rehash your high school experiences. If you have a graduate degree or are a graduate student, however, you should list both graduate and undergraduate course work. If you're still in school and graduation is more than a year away, indicate the number of credits you've earned through the most recent semester completed. Other activities, honors, and skills I'm always interested in—and impressed by—candidates who talk about books they've read and activities they've enjoyed. So make a list of all the sports, clubs, and other activities in which you've participated, inside or outside of school. For each activity, club or group, include: Ö Name and purpose. Ö Offices you held; special committees you formed, chaired, or participated in; or specific positions you played. Ö Duties and responsibilities of each role. Ö Key accomplishments. Ö Awards or honors you received. I would separately list all the awards and honors you've received from school(s), community groups, church groups, clubs, and so on. You may include awards from prestigious high schools (prep or professional schools) even if you're in graduate school or long out of college. Even if you're not applying for a job in the international arena, your ability to read, write, and/or speak additional languages can make you invaluable to employers in an increasing number of research and educational institutions and multinational companies. One year of college Russian won't cut it. But if you spent a year studying in Moscow—and can carry on a conversation like a native—by all means write it down.

Employers love veterans Many employers are impressed by the maturity of candidates who have served in the armed forces—they consider military service excellent management training for many civilian jobs. So if you've served in the armed forces, even for a short time, make sure you can discuss your experiences and how they support your professional aspirations. Be sure to include: Ö Final rank awarded. Ö Duties and responsibilities. Ö Citations and awards. Ö Details on specific training and/or any special schooling. Ö Special skills developed. Ö Key accomplishments.

And now for something completely different Recording and organizing all of this factual information about yourself is just the first step in "getting to know you." It is also important to ask yourself some of the questions that an interviewer may well ask you, not to prepare a memorized answer but to get a better understanding of your own personality. In fact, you can count on most interviewers asking some or even most of these questions in order to figure out who you are. It would be nice if you figured that out first!

Answering these questions should enable you to define both short- and long-term goals—personal, professional, and financial—and could even help you develop a road map to reach those dreams. Additionally, it will help you assess the fit between a company's culture, the job, the boss...and you. Unless you do this kind of analysis, on what basis will you evaluate job offers? As the old saying goes, if you don't know where you're going, any road will take you there.

So let's do a few lists to help you assess who you are, what's important to you, and what this analysis should tell you about the kind of company you want to work for. You'll quickly see that this is a far more detailed and completely different assessment than you were advised to do when collecting data for your resume. Write down your answers to the following questions, many of which you should expect an interviewer to ask: Questions about you as a person q Who are you? Describe your personality. q What are your values? What is important to you? q Which achievements did you enjoy most? Which are you proudest of? Be ready to tell the interviewer how these accomplishments relate to the position at hand. q What in your personal life causes you the most stress (relationships, money, time constraints, and so on)? What gives you the most pleasure? q What mistakes have you made? Why did they occur? What have you learned from them? What have you done to keep similar things from occurring again? q How well do you interact with authority figures—bosses, teachers, parents? Be ready to furnish specific examples. q What are your favorite games and sports? Are you overly competitive? Do you give up too easily? Are you a good loser or a bad winner? Do you rise to a challenge or back away from it? q What kinds of people are your friends? Do you associate only with people who are like you? Do you enjoy differences in others—or merely tolerate them? What are some things that have caused you to end friendships? What does this say about you? q If you were to ask a group of friends and acquaintances to describe you, what adjectives would they use? List all of them—the good and the bad. Why would people describe you this way? Are there specific behaviors, skills, achievements, or failures that seem to identify you in the eyes of others? What are they? Questions about you as a professional q What kinds of people do you like working with? What kinds do you dislike working with? q What are your goals and aspirations? q What would it take to transform yourself into someone who's passionate about every workday? q What are your passions? q How can you make yourself more marketable in today's competitive job market? q What are your major professional accomplishments? What competencies are your strongest calling cards? q What are your most notable failures? What did you learn from each? q What would your last boss say about your work ethic? What would your coworkers say about you? Your subordinates? q What specific things do you require in the job you're seeking—adventure, glamour, a bigger office, more money? Your strengths, abilities, and values The following list of descriptive adjectives (on page 52) should help you further define who you are, both professionally and personally. Circle those words or phrases that you believe describe you, and keep them in mind when assessing any job offer or any company and its attendant culture. These are all positive attributes, of one kind or another, to one company or another. After you've circled all of those you believe best describe you, ask your friends if they agree with your assessment— we aren't always the best judges of our own characters, are we?

Active Active in sports Active reader Active volunteer Adaptable Adventurous Ambitious Artistic Attractive Brave/heroic Calm Communicative Computer literate Confident Courteous Creative Decisive Dedicated Detail-oriented Directed Dynamic Economical Efficient Empathetic Ethical Excellent analytical skills Excellent math skills Experienced Extroverted Flexible Fluent in other languages Focused Goal-oriented Good delegating skills Good leadership skills Good listening skills Good mathematical skills Good negotiating skills Good presentation skills Good public speaking skills Good sense of humor Good team-building skills Good time management skills Good under pressure Good written communicator Graceful Handles stress well Hard-working High energy Highly educated (level?) Honest Introverted Learns from mistakes Left-brained Like people Likes to travel Logical Loves animals Loves children Loyal Makes friends easily Moral Musical Neat Obsessive Organized Passionate Passive Patient Perfectionist Performer Physically strong Precise Professional Quick-thinking Reacts well to authority Religious Responsible Right-brained Risk averse Risk taker Sales personality Self-motivated Sports fan Strong-willed Supportive of others Tenacious Welcomes change Well-groomed

What's the point?

The better you know yourself, the better you can sell yourself to a prospective employer when you're on the spot in an interview. From everything you've written down, you can now compile a list of your best features under the following headings: Ö My strongest skills. Ö My greatest areas of knowledge. Ö My greatest personality strengths. Ö The things I do best. Ö My key accomplishments. Then you can transform them into benefits for your prospective company. But you must also be ready to admit your shortcomings and what you are already doing about them. By answering some tough questions about the mistakes you have made—and the less-thanpositive feedback you've gotten—you can locate areas that need improvement. Do you need to develop new skills? Improve your relations with those in authority? If you have been thorough and brutally honest (and it may feel brutal!), you may find out things about yourself that you never knew. The more time and effort you invest in answering questions like these—while you have a cool head—the less you'll sweat once you're in the interviewer's hot seat. It's up to you. The importance of goals I've mentioned the importance of goals already. Now it's time to emphasize them. Short- and long-term goal setting must become a habit. Once a year, reevaluate not just the progress you're making toward your long-term goals, but whether they need to be tweaked, heavily modified, or even changed completely. Life is not static. Neither are your goals—they will (and should) change with circumstances, age, position, etc.

Remember that setting goals will not only help you define where you want to go, but what you need to know and do to get there. If you have decided that you eventually want to be Chief Financial Officer of a large corporation, you may well need an MBA or similar graduate degree. When do you plan to get it? Full or part time? If the latter, will the company allow a modified schedule so you can go to school while you work? Is there a tuition reimbursement plan? Is there already a program in place to which you can apply? It's equally important to make your goals realistic. There is nothing wrong with reaching for the stars, providing you have the right-size stepstool. If you aren't a high school graduate, you can aspire to becoming chairman of IBM, but your short-term goals better include some serious additional education! If you want to be a prize-winning author, passing a creative writing class might be a nice first step. Goals are realistic if there is a clear-cut path that you can follow to reach them. It may be a hard and long road, but if you truly believe you can actually reach its end with sufficient effort, then the goal is realistic. Even if a goal is completely unrealistic, I would not necessarily counsel you to drop it. First of all, who's to say it really is unrealistic? You may have little or no natural writing ability and couldn't draw a straight line if your life depended on it. Would I be willing to bet you probably won't become the creative director of one of the world's top three advertising agencies? Well, I'm a betting man, so I probably would take that bet. But the human spirit is an amazing thing. Who says with the right education, jobs, and practice that your goal, though seemingly unrealistic, couldn't eventually be realized? Even if it weren't, the additional educational and dedication certainly wouldn't hurt your career prospects! What if the goal is realistic but you are simply unwilling or unable to do what's necessary to reach it? Change it. Why kid yourself? While luck plays a factor in many careers, it is certainly not the only factor. The one common denominator of virtually any success story is hard work. If you aren't willing to work hard, almost any goal may be unrealistic.

4

So, Tell Me About Yourself

There it is—the granddaddy of all interview questions. And one that still—unbelievably—makes some of you stutter and stumble. It's really more of a request than a question, but it can put you on the spot as no other question can. And if you're unprepared for such an open-ended prelude to the series of standard questions about your skills, background, and aspirations you've been expecting, it can stop you dead in your tracks and earn you an immediate one-way ticket out of the interview. Why is this question a favorite of so many interviewers? Many consider it a nice icebreaker, giving them a chance to gauge initial chemistry, get a little insight into the cipher sitting before them (that would be you), and force you to do all the talking, for at least a couple of minutes. Should this time-tested question catch you unprepared? Certainly not. I guarantee that this will be one of the first three questions asked, often the very first one. So what happens if you do hem and haw your way through a disjointed, free-associating discourse that starts somewhere in Mrs. Mahamita's kindergarten class and, 10 minutes later, is just getting into the details of those eighth grade cheerleader tryouts? You may well tie the record for the shortest interview of the week.

Is the interviewer seeking specific clues (key words, body language)? Or, as I have secretly suspected of many an unseasoned interviewer, is she simply looking for the easiest way to get the ball rolling? It shouldn't matter to you. If you are prepared, you know this can be your golden opportunity to provide an answer that demonstrates four of the traits every interviewer is desperately searching for: intelligence, enthusiasm, confidence, and dependability. Getting Ready for the "Killer Question" q Complete your personal inventory. If you bypassed the work in Chapter 2, go back and do it now. q Distill your personal inventory into a compelling opening. Use specifics to paint a short-and-sweet picture of "you," in which you show yourself to be an enthusiastic and competent professional—the ideal candidate for the job. q Don't memorize it word for word. You want to sound fresh— not like you're reading from a set of internal cue cards. So know the content. Record yourself speaking it until it sounds sincere but spontaneous. q Include strong, positive phrases and words. You want to convey enthusiasm and confidence as well as knowledge and experience. What you don't know, you're eager to learn. q Use it to set the course of the interview. Anticipate that the "killer" will surface early in the interview, so be prepared to use it as an opportunity to steer the interview in the direction you want it to go. Fine-tune your response to give a positive slant to any potential negatives, such as apparent job-hopping and lack of related experience. Think about particular skills or accomplishments you want to showcase during that interview and prepare at least one good example of each. q End with the ball in the interviewer's court. By ending with a question, you get a much-deserved breather and, once again, demonstrate your involvement and enthusiasm.

So dig out the personal inventory you completed (I told you it would be an important prerequisite for making good use of this book) and study the items you listed under these headings: Ö My strongest skills. Ö My greatest areas of knowledge. Ö My greatest personality strengths. Ö The things I do best. Ö My key accomplishments. What do they want to hear? From this information, you will now construct a well-thought-out, logically sequenced summary of your experience, skills, talents, and schooling. A plus? If this brief introduction clearly and succinctly relates your experience to the requirements of the position. But be sure to keep it tightly focused—about 250 to 350 words, chock-full of specifics. It should take you no more than two minutes to recite an answer that features the following information: Ö Brief introduction. Ö Key accomplishments. Ö Key strengths demonstrated by these accomplishments. Ö Importance of these strengths and accomplishments to the prospective employer. Ö Where and how you see yourself developing in the position for which you're applying (tempered with the right amount of self-deprecating humor and modesty). Again, we're not talking War and Peace here. Two-hundredfifty to 350 words is about right (taking from 90 to 120 seconds to recite). Here's how Barb, a recent college graduate applying for C|an entry-level sales position, answered this question:

"I've always been able to get along with different types of people. I think it's because I'm a good talker and an even better listener. [Modestly introduces herself, while immediately laying claim to the most important skills a good salesperson should have.] "During my senior year in high school, when I began thinking seriously about which careers I'd be best suited for, sales came to mind almost immediately. In high school and during my summer breaks from college, I worked various part-time jobs at retail outlets. [Demonstrates industriousness and at least some related experience.] Unlike most of my friends, I actually liked dealing with the public. [Conveys enthusiasm for selling.] "However, I also realized that retail had its limitations, so I went on to read about other types of sales positions. I was particularly fascinated by what is usually described as consultative selling. I like the idea of going to a client you have really done your homework on and showing him how your products can help him solve one of his nagging problems, and then following through on that. [Shows interest and enthusiasm for the job.] "After I wrote a term paper on consultative selling in my senior year of college, I started looking for companies at which I could learn and refine the skills shared by people who are working as account executives. [Shows initiative both in researching the area of consultative selling to write a term paper and in then researching prospective companies.] "That led me to your company, Mr. Sheldon. I find the prospect of working with companies to increase the energy efficiency of their installations exciting. I've also learned some things about your sales training programs. They sound like they're on the cutting edge. [Gives evidence that she is an enthusiastic self-starter.] "I guess the only thing I find a little daunting about the prospect of working at Co-generation, Inc., is selling that highly technical equipment without a degree in engineering. By the way, what sort of support does your technical staff lend to the sales effort?" [Demonstrates that she is willing to learn what she doesn't know and closes by deferring to the interviewer's authority. By asking a question the interviewer must answer, Barb has also given herself a little breather. Now the conversational ball sits squarely in the interviewer's court.] Based on the apparent sincerity and detail of her answers, it's not a bad little "speech" of a mere 253 words, is it? Lack of eye contact. The interviewer is asking this question to find a little "chemistry," so give her the reaction she's looking for. Ö Lack of strong, positive phrases and words. It's the first question and, therefore, your first chance to get off on the right foot. Employ words that convey enthusiasm, responsibility, dedication, and success. If the very first answer is uninspired (especially an answer we all assume has been prepared and even rehearsed), I have almost never seen the interview improve very much. Many interviewers will simply cut their losses and move on to a more promising candidate. Ö A general, meandering response that fails to cite and highlight specific accomplishments. It's a plus if you have been savvy enough to "edit" what we all know is a well-rehearsed set speech to ensure that it's relevant to the job at hand. Many interviewers will consider it a minus if all they've heard are a bunch of generalities and few (or no) actual specifics to back them up. Ö No relevance to job or company. The interviewer did not ask you to tell her about your hobbies, dog, favorite ice cream flavor, or boy band. Some interviewers may give you the initial benefit of the doubt if your answer is too general or personal, but most will quickly probe for some job-related specifics. Ö Lack of enthusiasm. If you don't seem excited about interviewing for the job, most interviewers will not assume you'll suddenly "get religion" once you're hired.

Ö Nervousness. Some people are naturally nervous in the artificial and intimidating atmosphere of an interview, and most experienced interviewers won't consider this an automatic reason to have their secretary buzz them about that "emergency conference." But they'll wonder what may be lurking— a firing, a sexual harassment suit, something that isn't going to make their day. Ö Someone who asks a clarifying question, such as "What exactly do you want to know?" or "Which particular areas would you like me to talk about?" As I said earlier, I find it hard to believe anyone interviewing for anything has not anticipated that this question will be asked. What do you think the interviewer wants to know? Your opinion about Caitlyn Jenner's transition? She wants to know about your experience, skills, talents, and education, so answer the question, articulately and succinctly, and get ready for what comes next. Variations | What makes you special (unique, different)? | What five adjectives describe you best? | Rate yourself on a scale of one to 10. | How would you describe your character? | How would you describe your personality? | Tell me something you really don't want me to know. Despite the nuances, you should merely edit your "set piece" to respond to each of the first five questions in essentially the same way. So, although the first, fourth, and fifth questions appear to be more targeted, all five are really looking for the same information. The sixth variation, of course, is one of those curveballs that you didn't anticipate (or, at the very least, never thought it would be the very first question asked!). You are certainly not going to admit to your secret Hello Kitty addiction (or worse), so take a moment to think about (or dream up) a minor, non-job-related "secret" you can reveal.

Variations | Why are you here? | Why should I hire you? | Why should I consider you a strong candidate for this position? | What's better about you than the other candidates I'm interviewing? | What can you do for us that someone else can't? These are more aggressive questions, the tone of each a bit more forceful. An interviewer using one of these variations is clearly attempting to make you fully aware that you're on the hot seat. This may be a matter of his particular style, the introduction to his own brand of stress interview, or just a way to save time by seeing how you respond to pressure right from the get-go. The interviewer has "set you up," trying to separate the contenders from the also-rans with a single question. But he has actually given you a golden opportunity to display the extent of your pre-interview research. And if you haven't done any, you may well find yourself in a sea of hot water. Q: What are your strengths as an employee? What do they want to hear? To prepare for this question (as well as the variations just mentioned), pull out those sheets you labored over in Chapter 2 and write down the description of the position for which you're interviewing. This will help you clarify each specific job requirement in your mind. Then, match your strengths and accomplishments directly to the requirements of the job. Let's presume you have a singular skill for meeting even the most unreasonable deadlines. You are tenacious. Nothing can stop you. If "meeting deadlines" is a key job requirement, be sure to cite two or three pertinent examples from your experience. The more outrageous the deadline and herculean your efforts, the more important it is to bring to the interviewer's attention— at least twice.

Are there any gaps in your qualifications? Probably a few— especially if you're reaching for the challenge at the next level of your career. So now it's time to dig in and deal with the hard questions that you know will follow right on the tail of the ones above. Q: How would your best friend (college roommate, favorite professor, favorite boss, mother, family, etc.) describe you? What do they want to hear? Personally, I would start with the "best friend" variation if I were interviewing someone. Supposedly, that's who should know you best. So if you presented me with a half-baked picture of yourself, I'd shorten the interview—by about seven-eighths of an hour. Some interviewers prefer to ask you to describe your best friend and how you differ from one another. This is based on the untested but reasonable theory that if someone is your "best" friend, the two of you probably have quite a lot in common. Because you are supposedly describing your best friend, not yourself, some interviewers believe you may inadvertently reveal character insights (i.e., flaws) you would otherwise prefer to conceal. So, take pains to describe a person the interviewer would find it easy to hire. All of the other variations on this question may be used by experienced interviewers to home in on specific times in your life and career (college, high school, last job) or just to get a fuller picture of you. What your mother or father would say, for example, may give the interviewer a clear illustration of the kind of environment in which you were raised. Variations | How would someone who doesn't like you describe you? You're trying hard to avoid introducing any negatives, so your wonderful interviewer is offering a helping hand. Despite her offer to let you wallow in a pond of despair, just keep accentuating your positive qualities. You can always claim that the other person doesn't like you because of them.

Q: What do you want to be doing five years from now? What do they want to hear? Are the company's goals and yours compatible? Are you looking for fast or steady growth in a position the interviewer knows is a virtual dead end? Are you requesting more money than he can ever pay? How have your goals and motivations changed as you have matured and gained work experience? If you've recently become a manager, how has that promotion affected your future career outlook? If you've realized you need to acquire or hone a particular skill, how and when are you planning to do so? This question is not as popular as it once was, since the pace of change at many corporations continues to increase so rapidly. You are more likely to be asked to concentrate on a much tighter time frame: "What will you be able to accomplish during your first 90 (100, 180) days on the job?" Naturally, you want a position of responsibility in your field. But you don't want to give the impression that you're a piranha waiting to feed on the guppies in your new department. So, start humbly: "Well, that will ultimately depend on my performance on the job, and on the growth and opportunities offered by my employer." Then toot your own horn a bit: "I've already demonstrated leadership characteristics in all of the jobs I've held, so I'm very confident that I will take on progressively greater management responsibilities in the future. That suits me fine. I enjoy building a team, developing its goals, and then working to accomplish them. It's very rewarding." In other words, you want "more"—more responsibility, more people reporting to you, more turf, even more money. A general answer (as above) is okay, but don't be surprised when an interviewer asks the obvious follow-up questions (using the answer to the above question as a guide):

Ö Tell me about the last team you led. Ö Tell me about the last project your team undertook. Ö What was the most satisfying position you've held, and why? Ö If I told you our growth was phenomenal and you could go as far as your abilities would take you, where would that be, and how quickly? If you answer "your job." Everyone is tired of that trite response by now. If you refuse to offer more than a "general" answer—that is, no real specific goals—no matter how hard the interviewer probes for more. Your inability or unwillingness to cite specific, positive goals may give the impression, warranted or not, that you have not taken the time to really think about your future, which makes it impossible for the interviewer to assess whether there's a fit between his goals and yours. If you insist you want to be in the same job for which you're applying. (Unless it is a dead-end job and the interviewer would be pleased as punch if someone actually stayed longer than three weeks, unlike the last 14 people to hold the position.) Any answer that reveals unrealistic expectations. A savvy candidate should have some idea of the time it takes to climb the career ladder in a particular industry or even in a company. Someone hoping to go from receptionist to CEO in two years will, of course, scare off most interviewers, but any expectations that are far too ambitious could give them pause. If a law school grad, for example, seeks to make partner in four years—when the average for all firms is seven and, for this one, 10—it will make even novice interviewers question the extent and effectiveness of your preinterview research. There's nothing wrong with being ambitious and confident beyond all bounds, but a savvy interviewee should temper such boundless expectations during the interview. Most interviewers are aware that some candidates do "break the rules" successfully, but they will get a little nervous around people exhibiting unbridled ambition! If you have made an interviewer worry that her company couldn't possibly deliver on the promises you seem to want to hear, you can expect a follow-up question: "How soon after you're hired do you think you can contribute to our success?" Even someone with a tremendous amount of pertinent experience knows full well that each company has its own particular ways of doing things and that the learning curve may be days, weeks, or many months, depending on circumstances. So any candidate—but especially an overly ambitious young person—who blithely assures an interviewer she'll be productive from day one is cause for concern. The interviewer is really trying to assess, in the case of an inexperienced person, how "trainable" you are, and you've just told him you think you already know it all! Not a good start. For some reason, some applicants fail to remember that this is an interview, not a conversation in a bar or with friends. As a result, they rattle off some remarkable responses that can only be deemed "fantasies"—to be retired, own their own business, live on the beach, and so on—though why they would think these answers pertinent to their job search is beyond me. I would seriously discourage ever answering this question in such a manner. Variations | What are your long-term goals? | Have you recently established any new objectives or goals? | What do you want to do with your life? | What do you want to be when you grow up? These questions provide you with an opportunity to demonstrate how your goals and motivations have changed as you've matured and gained valuable work experience. If you've recently become a manager, talk about how that experience has affected your career outlook for the future. If you've realized that you must sharpen a particular skill to continue growing, tell the interviewer what you're doing about it. Q: If you could change one thing about your personality just by snapping your fingers, what would it be and why? What do they want to hear? That you have weaknesses—of course you do!—but none that are lethal. Conventional career advice has been to cite a "weakness" that you can easily show is really a strength: "You know, sir, I just work too hard. I have to take more time off than just Sunday from 5 to 7." Sure you do. An answer most interviewers would find acceptable would reveal a weakness that you've already corrected or, in a slight redirection of the question, a mistake you made in a previous job and the lesson(s) you learned from it. In both cases, you would be turning a negative question into a positive response. My strategy was always to cite a particular skill or qualification that I obviously lacked...but one that wasn't remotely needed in the job I was interviewing for. Identifying a weakness that is job-related or, worse, essential to the job at hand (for example, the inability to work with others when the job for which you are interviewing is highly team based). Citing a weakness that is so basic or stupid that the interviewer has to wonder if that's the biggest thing (she did say one thing) you could change. Variations | Tell me about the one thing in your life you're proudest of. | Tell me about the worst decision you ever made. | Tell me about the one thing in your life you're most ashamed of. | What's your greatest weakness?

The first puts you on comfortable turf—a positive question you can answer positively. The latter three questions force you to turn a negative question into a positive answer, and, because any negative question invites the unwary to descend into a sea of recriminations ("Working for that last jerk, let me tell you!"), it is a potential quagmire. In all cases, the interviewer is inviting conversation but not as one way and open-ended as in earlier questions. These might well be follow-up questions if "Tell me about yourself" or something similar didn't "open everything up" as much as the interviewer hoped it would. You should, therefore, take them as a sign that you've yet to tell the interviewer what he or she wants to hear. Q: What does "success" mean to you? What do they want to hear? You should offer a balanced answer to this question, citing personal as well as professional examples. If your successes are exclusively job-related, an interviewer may wonder if you actually have a life. However, if you blather on about your personal goals and accomplishments, you may seem uncommitted to striving for success on the job. Strike a balance and talk about success in terms such as these: "I have always enjoyed supervising a design team. In fact, I've discovered that I'm better at working with other designers than designing everything myself. Unlike a lot of the people in my field, I'm also able to relate to the requirements of the manufacturing department. "So, I guess I'd say success means working with others to come up with efficient designs that can be up on the assembly line quickly. Of course, the financial rewards of managing a department give me the means to travel during my vacations. That's the thing I love most in my personal life."

If the interviewer identifies any of the following problems from your answer, you're already on thin ice and better race back to shore: Ö Incompatibility of his or her goals and yours. Ö Lack of focus in your answer. Ö Too general an answer, with no examples of what successes you have already achieved. Ö Too many personal examples. Ö Too many job-related examples. Q: What does "failure" mean to you? What do they want to hear? A specific example to demonstrate what you mean by "failure," not a lengthy philosophical discussion more suited to a Bergman film than an interview. This question offers an experienced interviewer the opportunity to delve into mistakes and bad decisions, not a happy topic as far as you're concerned. He is looking for honesty, a clear analysis of what went wrong, a willingness to admit responsibility (with a small plus if it's obvious you're taking responsibility for some aspects that weren't your fault), and evidence that you are determined to change what caused it (or examples to show how it's already been transformed). "Failure is not getting the job done when I have the means to do so. For example, once I was faced with a huge project. I should have realized at the outset that I didn't have the time. I must have been thinking there were 48 hours in a day! I also didn't have the knowledge I needed to do it correctly. Instead of asking some of the other people in my department for help, I blundered through. That won't ever happen to me again if I can help it!" A noncommital, nonspecific answer that forces the interviewer to ask more and more follow-up questions to get any kind of handle on what makes you tick.

Always remember why the interviewer is asking you such openended questions: to get you talking, hopefully so you reveal more than you would have if he or she had asked a more pointed question. So answer such questions clearly, succinctly, and specifically—but avoid any temptation to "confess" your many sins. Variations | What does "achievement" mean to you? | What does "challenge" mean to you? | What does "problem" mean to you? | What does "impossible" mean to you? | What does "growth" mean to you? Q: What would you say if I told you our interview is over? Well, isn't that a kick in the teeth? Maybe your first or second answers were so poor the interviewer is trying to save some time and just get you out the door. Maybe she is baiting you, giving you an opportunity to rise to the challenge of her rejection. Maybe she just wants to get back to work. Whatever the reason, you must be prepared to confront her aggression with a calm question of your own: "I'm sorry you feel that way. I thought I clearly expressed my passion for this position and why I believe I am very qualified for it. What part of my answer disappointed you?" Variations | What if I told you I thought this interview was off to a poor start? | Sorry, you haven't convinced me you are remotely qualified for this position. We should end this interview now. | Would you like to start over? You're not doing very well. | I only have five more minutes. Why should I hire you?

Tips for Convincing the Interviewer You're a Great Catch q Do your homework. Find out as much as you can about the company and how the position for which you're interviewing contributes to its goals. q Demonstrate experience—and exude confidence. Give the interviewer strong answers using concrete examples that are relevant to the position you are after. q Be humble. Convey the impression that you have the ability to succeed should opportunities present themselves. But avoid giving the impression that you're a fire-breathing workaholic ready to succeed no matter what (or whom) the cost. q Appear firm, but not dictatorial. When you talk about your management philosophy, let the interviewer know that you are able to delegate, keep track of each person's progress, and stay on top of your own work. q Talk about growth. Tell the interviewer how you've grown in each of the jobs you've held and how your career goals have changed as a result. q Admit your failures. Concentrate on what you've learned from past failures, using examples that show how you've changed as a result of them. q Showcase your successes. Make sure to position yourself as a professional with a satisfying personal life.

Think in terms of what...and why. As you trumpet your successes—or mumble about your failures—stress the positive lessons you learned from each situation and how you've already applied them (or plan to in your next position). q Don't exaggerate. Your accomplishments and responsibilities should speak for themselves. If you felt you lacked opportunities to make a mark in a past position, say so. But don't bend the truth—there are too many ways a savvy interviewer can unmask you. Don't learn the hard way—it will probably cost you the job! q Don't appear desperate...even if your last job was months ago. Some interviewers will equate "desperate" with "cheap to hire," presuming they want to hire you at all. But don't come across as smug either. Concentrate on expressing your genuine interest and enthusiasm for the opportunities inherent in the job on offer. q Avoid the negative. You want the interviewer to associate nothing but positive words, thoughts, and deeds with you. q Make the best of your current position. Convey that you are a positive person who always makes the best of any situation. The worse your actual situation, the better you'll look. q Build a vocabulary of action words and use them consistently in your resume, cover letter, follow-up letters and during interviews.

Don't get carried away. Only the most annoying people find it easy to talk about themselves in a flattering way. And that's what you'll be doing on the interview— constantly tooting your own horn, until even you will want to change the tune. q Stress the traits companies are looking for. I mean enthusiasm, confidence, energy, dependability, honesty. Formulate answers that suggest these characteristics. Think about what you would want in an ideal employee if you owned a company. Wouldn't you want a problemsolver? A team player? Someone who is enthusiastic about working hard to achieve goals? q Be creative. A friend of mine had to work his way through college. Rather than participate in low- or no-pay internship programs or extracurricular activities, he pumped gas and stocked supermarket shelves during the summers. So when asked why he hadn't had any internships, he was ready to reply: "I wish I'd had more time to write for the school paper. Whenever I wasn't studying, I pretty much had to work to pay for college. But I learned a number of things from the jobs I held that most people learn only after they've been in their careers for a while, such as how to work with other people and how to manage my time effectively."

5

Questions About Your Education

The more work experience you have, the less anyone will care about what you did in college, even if you attended Podunk rather than Princeton. As important as particular courses and extracurricular leadership positions may have been a decade ago, no amount of educational success can take the place of solid, realworld, on-the-job experience. But if your diploma is so fresh the ink could stain your fingers and your only (summer) job was intimately involved with salad ingredients, then the questions in this chapter are directed to you, the relatively inexperienced candidate facing that age-old catch-22: You need experience to get the job, but how can you get experience if you can't get a job? So it's back to "Creative Thinking 101." On your resume and in your interviews, you'll attempt to "upgrade" your experience, no matter how little or minor, while avoiding the temptation to blatantly transform a summer job at the local hot dog stand or on the beach into what sounds like a divisional vice presidency. How are you going to accomplish this? You want to portray yourself as a well-rounded person who, in addition to getting decent grades, demonstrated desirable traits—leadership, team building, writing, communicating—either through extracurricular activities, internships, and/or part-time work experience.

If you weren't a member of many official school clubs or teams, talk about other activities you engaged in during college. Did you work part time? Tutor other students? Work for extra course credit? What you've been doing—whatever you have been doing— should demonstrate a pattern that bears at least some passing relation to the job at hand. What you did during your summers, unless it was a pertinent internship or part-time job, is virtually irrelevant. You chose a major, particular courses, clubs, and activities—most interviewers will want to know the reasons why you made those particular choices. That will reveal to them where your "real" interests lie...no matter what perfect "objective" you've branded atop your resume. Q: What extracurricular activities were you involved in? What do they want to hear? Most interviewers are seeking a candidate who can illustrate industriousness, not just someone who did enough to eke by. They're expecting enthusiasm, confidence, energy, dependability, honesty. A problem solver. A team player. Someone who's willing to work hard to achieve difficult but worthy goals. Activities that bear some relationship to the job/industry— for example, a college newspaper editor applying for a job in newspaper, book, or magazine publishing. Activities that show a healthy balance. You are probably a top candidate for a wide variety of jobs if you participated in one or more sports and a cultural club (chess, theater, etc.) and a political club and you worked part-time, as opposed to someone whose sole focus was on a sport or cause, no matter how illustrious his or her athletic or other achievements. If you're able to demonstrate the ability to manage multiple priorities (let's not forget coursework and maybe a part-time job here) and good time-management skills.

If you've spent an inordinate amount of time doing things outside of class but your GPA (Grade Point Average) indicates you spent too little time concentrating in class. (Anything below a B average should lead you to expect a whole series of follow-up questions, forcing you to explain why.) If you have seemingly tried every activity at least once and have demonstrated no clear direction, most interviewers will not assume you'll suddenly change on the job. Never think a joke is a good answer: "Well, Mr. Johns, I didn't do much more than drink beer on weekends." I'm probably more appreciative of good jokes than the next guy, but an interview is simply the wrong place and the wrong time to channel Colbert. Even if you're funny, most interviewers will probably question the common sense of anyone who thinks sitting across from their desk applying for a job is the right time and place to try out a new stand-up routine. Variations | What made you choose those activities? | Which ones did you most enjoy? Why? | Which ones did you least enjoy? Why? | Which ones do you regret not choosing? Why? The interviewer posing questions like these is just trying to get a handle on how you think, how you make choices and decisions, and how flexible or inflexible you seem to be in those choices. Q: Why did you choose your college? Why did you choose your major? Why did you choose your minor?

Which courses did you like most? Least? What do they want to hear? If you are a recent college graduate, some interviewers may substitute this series of questions for the ubiquitous "So, tell me about yourself"—your college experience is probably a good measure of "yourself."

If you were a liberal arts major, talk about the skills you developed in some of your courses: writing ability, researching and analytical skills, debating, language and communication skills. Assuming that you took courses related to the job at hand, focus only on those that are career oriented. Don't feel handicapped if you majored in something non-technical or non-professional. Most interviewers, even those offering fairly technical jobs, expect to spend an inordinate amount of their time cajoling an endless line of history, English, and French lit majors to explain how their college education prepared them for a sales/marketing/management/executive position. What was your thought process? Did you choose a major because it was the easiest? Because it had specific relevance to other interests (as demonstrated by consistent volunteer/work/ activities)? Because you analyzed the job market and took courses to prepare for a particular career/industry? Just because it was there? What other majors or minors did you consider? And why did you choose one and reject the others? If you are being interviewed for a highly technical job—engineering, science, programming, etc.—the interviewer should reasonably expect that you majored in engineering, chemistry, or computer science, and that your major and even minor coursework is pertinent (with the exception of someone like my friend Andy, who majored in astrophysics at MIT...and minored in theater). It will probably be a plus if you demonstrated a particular interest in chemistry or computers or mechanical engineering while still in high school. Talk about the skills you developed, especially in courses you didn't necessarily like or want to take. I like to hear that a candidate did well in a course she really didn't care for. I seem to spend an inordinate amount of time doing things I don't care for, but I still must do them to the best of my ability. When I interview people, I'm seeking someone with the same attitude.

When talking about particular courses, develop answers that focus on the subject, not the workload or the professor's personality. Talking about past troubles with an authority figure will introduce a possible negative into your current candidacy. And complaining about too much work is not the best way to impress any prospective boss. Interviewers don't take kindly to freshly minted graduates who expect to start at a salary higher than their own. So acknowledge that you are well aware that despite your summa cum laude credentials, you probably have less job-related knowledge than the senior person in the mailroom. Humility is an attractive trait at times, especially when it's well deserved: "I know this position has its share of unpleasant duties, but I'm sure everyone who's had this job before me has learned a lot by doing them." Blaming a professor, even tangentially, for a bad grade or experience will give many interviewers pause—do you have problems with authority figures? Complaining about the workload of a course, semester, or year. Interviewers are seeking industriousness, not laziness. There are interviewers out there—and I'm one of them—who go out of their way to describe in excruciating detail the worst or most mind-numbingly boring aspects of the job. A successful candidate shouldn't be fooled into expressing any negative reaction—(even a raised eyebrow when "garbage detail" is being discussed! Variations | Why did you change majors? Change minors? Drop that course? Add that course? What do they want to hear? Again, what was your thought process? The change may well be considered a positive—if you explain and justify it well— unless, of course, it clearly was to eliminate a difficult major for an easier one, a stratagem to take more classes with a girlfriend, or something equally superfluous. If you have changed majors, even more than once, you must be ready to admit that you simply didn't have all the answers when you were 19. (Don't worry, neither did the interviewer.) I suspect many interviewers would find such candor refreshing and realistic. After all, how many high school seniors know that eventually they will (or want to) become accountants, or hospital administrators, or loading dock foremen, or, for that matter, interviewers for Human Resources? But you should be prepared to show how your other studies contributed to making you the best candidate for the job. Q: Why are you applying for a job in a field other than your major? What do they want to hear? Life doesn't always turn out according to our plans. Especially when you're young, changes in direction are common. Changes are hard enough to live through without getting grilled about them. But when the interviewer asks about one of your 180-degree turns, you've got to respond. If you're applying for a retail management position and your degree is in geology, there's a good chance that you'll be asked this question. But count on it—it's not the first time this employer has encountered someone like you. In today's job market, changing careers is common, and there's nothing unique about going into a field other than the one you majored in. So what do you do? You know you've piqued the employer's interest enough to get an interview, right? So relax and answer the question. Keep it brief and positive: You've reexamined your career goals. You enjoy customer contact, the competitive nature of sales, and the varied management responsibilities required in retail, and you've decided it's the career you want to pursue. And, oh yeah (perhaps with a sheepish grin), there are only 142 new jobs in geology this year—and you didn't get any of them! Then it may be a good idea to pause and ask, "Have I answered your question?" Give the interviewer an opportunity to express concerns about your qualifications. If he has any, be prepared to explain how the skills required in your degree field transfer to the field in which you're seeking employment. You can use the same strategy with your prior work experience. Are there particular things a geologist must learn that directly translate into retail management? Particular skills? I don't know, but you certainly better be ready to talk about them. Just because many students who major in more esoteric areas are, by definition, ill-prepared for some specific jobs, and because many people now change jobs, careers, and even industries more and more, that does not mean that many interviewers will not make you sell them on how your learning will benefit them. Q: If you were starting college tomorrow, what courses would you take? What do they want to hear? Be prepared to detail changes you would have made in your course selections that would have made you a better candidate for this job. Should you have taken more marketing courses, an accounting course, a statistics seminar? At the same time, don't be afraid to admit that it took you a little while to find the right course of study. A bit of candor is fine, but avoid offering a dissertation involving a wholesale change of major, minor, and hair color. C| Consider this question a good opportunity to describe how courses that are completely unrelated to this or any other "real-world" career nevertheless were valuable in your development. Don't claim you would have gone away to school so you could have dated more. D Don't answer, "Same courses, but this time I'd pass."

Don't answer in a way that clearly implies you don't understand the purpose of the question. You have been given an opportunity to show you know what the job entails and, because of that understanding, to declare you would have taken more pertinent courses while dropping that 17th century Chinese literature course like a hot chop stick. Q: What did you learn from the internships on your resume? What do they want to hear? No company really believes that you're going to hit the ground running right out of college or graduate school. Training and experience will be necessary to make you productive. So, as a relatively inexperienced candidate, you can expect an interviewer to do a bit of probing—trying to determine how "trainable" you are. Stress how the real-world internship experience you've had complemented your academic training. But never pretend that college is where you learned the "secret of life." No interviewer is going to react favorably to someone who acts like he or she knows it all. If you are able to show how the real internship experience you had complemented your academic training. Pertinent internships that tie in directly to your new job/career. Well-thought-out answers that demonstrate consistent career concerns. Good recommendations from internship supervisors. If you sincerely believe—and, worse, actually tell the interviewer—that college is where you learned the "secret of life." No internships in a field in which they are de rigueur.

Internship(s) in an unrelated field (especially if it ties in with your courses/activities, indicating that your real area of interest lies elsewhere). Poor or no recommendation from your internship supervisor or a negative reaction from you about its value. (Even if your internship turned out to test nothing more than your coffeemaking skills, you should never introduce such a negative into the interview.) Variations | Why are there no internships on your resume? | Why weren't any of your internships paid? | Would you repeat each of your internships? | Why did you pick those particular internships? | Why did you feel the need to do an internship? | Have you ever shadowed a professional in this field? Q: In what courses did you get the worst grades? Why? How do you think that will affect your performance on this job? What do they want to hear? Many companies will ask to see copies of your college transcripts if you don't have work experience. So you might as well spill the beans now! If you flunked every accounting course, you're probably not applying for an accounting job, right? Hopefully, you can blame bad grades you received in some of your electives on the amount of time and effort you were putting into your major. Do interviewers expect that every interviewee is a straight-A student and, therefore, will have a hard time answering this question? Not in my world. So the answer to the first part of the question is less important than the explanation and how you handle introducing a negative: "Yes, sir, I flunked statistical analysis, but it was completely outside my major and, as far as I know, has nothing to do with the job you're offering."

If you really can't answer the question because you didn't get any bad grades! If you satisfactorily explain the one or two less-thanstellar grades.

If a poor grade was in an elective course, blame the extra time you spent on your major (in which, of course, you did great). If you blew a single major course, perhaps outside activities were to blame (and you have a ready explanation for placing such activities ahead of good grades). Too many C's and D's to count. No reasonable explanation, leading an interviewer to assume that you simply didn't care or aren't all that bright. A choice that you made based on reasons most interviewers would question. Although it may have been quite exciting and educational to devote a significant amount of time to getting your friend elected student body president, were a plethora of D's a viable trade-off? Variations | Are grades a good measure of ability? | Why didn't you get better grades? | Why are your grades so erratic? | What happened that semester (year) when your grades sunk? What do they want to hear? Again, if your grades were great, you should be suitably proud; if they weren't, hopefully there were mitigating circumstances: work, an unusual opportunity, a family crisis, whatever. But if you fail to take responsibility for a poor performance, most interviewers would consider it a big thumbs down. Whatever you do, don't become defensive. This will lead most interviewers to wonder whether you actually made a choice or simply did something without thinking of the consequences.

Don't be afraid to say you'll need help. And when you do need help, make sure that the interviewer knows you'll ask for it. Not many companies are looking for—or expect to find—a 22-year-old know-it-all. If you are a 22-year-old know-it-all, keep it to yourself. q Admit that you don't have all the answers. Or begin a lot of your answers with "I think..." or "From what I know about the industry...." q Don't appear squeamish at the idea of going through the school of hard knocks. Tell the interviewer, "Sure, I know this position has its share of unpleasant duties, but I'm sure everyone who's had this job before me has learned a lot by doing them." q If it took a little time for you to find your direction, admit it. Nobody has all the answers at 18 or 19. Most interviewers will not be surprised that you changed your major as an undergraduate. Show how your other studies contribute to making you the best candidate. q Don't answer any question about who paid for your educational expenses or about any outstanding educational loans you may be carrying. Go ahead and play up the fact that you received a full academic scholarship or were industrious enough to work your way through school, if you want to. But by law, you don't have to say any more. For more detail on how to recognize and deflect illegal questions,

6

Questions About Your Experience

It should come as no surprise that most interview questions will focus on your previous work experience. You've bid your alma mater adieu, either last decade or last week, so what have you done out there in the real world? Many employers think that your past is a "prologue" to your future performance. If you do have some deep, dark character flaw, they figure it must have shown up already! So be prepared to be thoroughly grilled about every job you've ever had, especially the last two or three. Stay positive through it all. And don't forget about pertinent volunteer experience, even if it was unpaid—it may be a good way to "add" a skill or qualification you haven't been able to attain on the job. Let's look at some of the questions you're likely to face. Q: Tell me about your last three positions. Explain what you did, how you did it, the people you worked for, and the people you worked with. What do they want to hear? Whew! This is a scattergun approach, in part designed to see how well you organize what could be a lot of data into a brief, coherent overview of three, five, 10 or more years' experience. Interviewers who ask this question, or one like it, are trying to flesh out your resume, catch inconsistencies, create a road map for the far more detailed inquiries to follow, and evaluate how well you "edit" your answer to match your experience and skills to the requirements of the job at hand. If you can boast pertinent experience and skills in a brief, coherent, positive answer. If you are cognizant of the importance of relating your experience and skills to the interviewer's job requirements. A clear pattern upward: Increased responsibility, authority, money, subordinates, skill level, and so on. Asking the interviewer my least favorite question: "What exactly do you want to know?" (Answer: What I just asked for!) Any answer that is inconsistent with the facts on your resume (dates, duties, titles). You would think no one would refer to a job that doesn't appear on his or her resume, but it happens all the time. (And if you hint at such a problem, here's how a good interviewer will make you sweat: "Your resume says that you were working at during 2002, but you just said you were working at . How do you explain that?") I'll admit to being part of the stupidest interview ever undertaken by an otherwise smart, reasonably experienced person. I spent the first five years after graduating from Princeton trying to be a full-time writer without actually starving to death. The only way to accomplish that was to work a series of short-term, parttime jobs (often two or three at once) while I frantically turned out short stories, newspaper and magazine articles, plays, screenplays, and, eventually, books, some of which I actually got paid for. How many different jobs did I have? Dozens. Some lasted a day, some months, one nearly two years. But the only one that appeared on my resume was the twoyear stint at a trade association, because my supervisor graciously agreed to back up my white lie and allow me to claim that it was full time—for five years.

Within ten minutes of sitting down in front of the interviewer for a major magazine company, I was blithely discoursing on what I had learned at two or three of these other jobs. Yes, that's right, the ones that officially didn't exist. I finally realized what I had done…a minute or so after the interviewer. At about the same time, the interviewer and I both tumbled to the reality—I wasn't getting this job or, for that matter, any other potential job at that magazine company. We parted, amiably, though I felt like a small poodle that had been pulled through one too many mud puddles. So don't torpedo your candidacy by detailing jobs, responsibilities, and skills that don't "officially" exist. It worked for me! Don't complain in any way, shape, or form about bosses, subordinates, or coworkers. Most interviewers will fail to be impressed by anyone attempting to blame everyone else for his or her failures. Even it you weren't at fault, any transfer of blame will not be deemed a positive. Most interviewers will grill you about lateral moves (why didn't you get promoted?) and, even more so, about obvious demotions. You'd better have a very good explanation ready. Q: What was your favorite job? Why? What do they want to hear? A description of the job the interviewer is discussing. Presuming that you have to acknowledge that your favorite job differs from the job at hand in a couple of very specific, perhaps even important ways, you can still recover if you can explain why and how you have changed so that the current job is much more appropriate for you now. Any answer that inadvertently reveals the kind of job you're really seeking—obviously not the one being offered: My favorite job was at WPRB radio. It was very loose and informal and there was little supervision, which I really enjoyed. I had the freedom to program my own shows with little or no interference and only had to put in 20 hours a week to actually get my work done, so the rest of the time I could write or think up new creative ideas." This sounds like a reasonable answer...if only you weren't applying for a job assisting four high-powered businesspeople who are always on deadline and require ten hours a week overtime at a highly structured and very rigid old-line firm. It's not a problem if your last job offered some travel and this one doesn't, or the previous position offered more varied tasks and this one is more highly focused. But it is a problem if your answer fails to take into account what the current job entails, which will indicate to many interviewers a lack of pre-interview research or the simple inability to realize the importance of matching past experience to his or her needs. Q: Tell me about the best boss you ever had. Tell me about the worst one. What do they want to hear? Talk about a loaded question! If you're asked to talk about the best boss you ever had, you could try for an on-the-spot description of the hiring manager sitting across the desk from you. But as a rule of thumb, most companies want to hear that you most enjoyed working for someone who was interested in helping you learn and grow, involved in monitoring your progress, and generous about giving credit when and where it was due. I hope you've had the chance to work for someone like that! Now, what do you say about your worst boss? Don't get carried away with venomous accusations. They may serve only to introduce doubt about your own competence or ability to get along with other people. For example, if you level the charge of "favoritism," the interviewer might wonder why your boss liked other employees more than you. If you complain about a boss who was always looking over your shoulder, the interviewer might wonder whether it was because you couldn't be trusted to complete a task accurately, on budget, on time—or all three. If you understand that this question offers you an opportunity to accentuate your own experiences, accomplishments, and qualities. There are bad bosses out there, but a savvy candidate should be able to put a supervisor's failures in a positive context. If you say your boss was "stingy with his knowledge," you are accentuating your desire to learn. In the same vein, saying that a manager was "uninvolved" could indicate your desire to work within a cohesive team. Just prepare—and practice—your responses ahead of time. Any negativity. Any attempt to blame the boss for your failures: "You know, I had to really work hard to learn how to sell spice racks in the South Pacific, but it sure didn't help that my boss had never sold a darn thing to anyone. She seemed to think that everything I did was wrong and constantly called me out of the field for evaluations. I spent so much time filling out unnecessary reports for her and attending meetings to discuss why I wasn't reaching my unrealistic quota, that I never had a chance to succeed. I hope my new boss just leaves me alone." Q: Looking back now, is there anything you could have done to improve your relationship with that supervisor? Of course there is (presuming you are smart enough to grasp the life raft the interviewer just flung overboard). The work experience you've had since has shown you how to better accept criticism. Now that you have a better understanding of the pressures your supervisors are under, you can more successfully anticipate their needs. Use this opportunity to demonstrate your experience, perceptiveness, and maturity .

"Nah, not with that dumb so-and-so. He reveled in our misery. I'm glad we put sugar in his gas tank!" Q: What were the most memorable accomplishments at your last job? In your career? What do they want to hear? Focus on your most recent accomplishments—in your current position or the job you had just prior to this one. But make sure they are relevant to the position for which you're interviewing. For example, a friend of mine who had been an editor for years answered this question by talking at length about the times she'd been asked to write promotional copy for the marketing department. She was trying to change careers so she deliberately tried to shift the interviewer's attention from her editing experience to her accomplishments as a marketing copywriter. It's also wise to think about why you were able to achieve these peaks in your career. For example: "I really stopped to listen to what my customers wanted, rather than just trying to sell them." "I realized I needed to know a lot more about Subchapter-S corporations, so I enrolled in a tax seminar." This type of response tells the interviewer you give a great deal of thought to how you will reach your goals rather than blindly plunging ahead in their general direction. By letting the interviewer know that you are in the practice of regularly assessing your shortcomings, you show that you are better able to find the means to overcome them. Bragging about accomplishments that have nothing to do with the requirements for this job. Citing (proudly or otherwise) frivolous, meaningless, minor, or dubious accomplishments: I finally managed to get out of bed every morning and get to work on time." "I personally raised $25 for the volunteer fire department." "I successfully typed all my boss's correspondence the same week it was handed to me, even though I had to work all day on it." Q: What is the biggest failure you've had in your career? What steps have you taken to make sure something like that doesn't happen again? What do they want to hear? In this situation, it would be foolhardy to produce a detailed log of your every shortcoming, misstep, and misdeed. But it would be equally silly to pretend you're perfect and have never experienced failure in the course of your career, education, or life. The best approach is to admit to one weakness or failure— make it a good one!—and then talk about the steps you are taking (or have taken) to make sure that you'll never fail in that way again. What makes a failure not so bad or a weakness acceptable? Good question! Choose any deficiency that might be considered a plus in a slightly different light. For example: Ö You have a tendency to take on too much by yourself. You're trying to solve this problem by delegating more. Ö You're impatient with delays. You're trying to better understand every step of the process a product must go through so you can anticipate holdups in the future. Ö You've realized you're a workaholic. But you're doing your best to remedy your "condition" by reading books on time management. Try to think of a failure that took place relatively early in your career and/or one that would seem completely unrelated to the work you would be performing for your new employer.

Don't ever admit to any personal quality that might hamper job performance, such as procrastination, laziness, or lack of concentration. Acknowledge a failure for which you do not appear to be fully responsible. (When I'm interviewing someone, the way a successful candidate scores the most points is to make it obvious she wasn't fully responsible for an admitted failure but is ready, nevertheless, to shoulder all the blame.) If you must cite a job-related failure, be prepared to convince the interviewer that you now recognize what your error was and offer concrete examples that illustrate the lessons you've learned. Claiming that you've never failed. Citing a non-work related failure. Your inability to offer any evidence that you are prepared to take responsibility for whatever failure is cited nor any proof that any changes were made as a result. Don't declare, "That can never happen again." This is an unrealistic assessment that will call your judgement into question. Never confess a huge work-related weakness: "I've always hated my bosses, every one. But I think I'll like you!" Variations | What's your greatest weakness? | What's the worst decision you ever made?

| What's the dumbest thing you ever did? | What would you say is the biggest problem you've so far failed to overcome? | What don't you want me to know about you? | What aren't you telling me?

A good interviewer will, based on the answers to questions like these, continue to probe and put you on the spot, searching for details, details, and more details. If, for example, you say your greatest weakness is a fear of delegating because it always seems you can get it done faster and better yourself, you might be asked, "Tell me about the last time you should have delegated but didn't. What happened? Would you do it that way again? Would you do it differently today?" Such probing can also help the interviewer assess your character: how you react to stress; how well you handle pressure, failure, or success; your own standards of "success" and "failure"; and how willing you are to assume responsibility, especially for decisions or outcomes that weren't your fault. Q: Have you managed people in any of the positions you've held? What do they want to hear? Moving up in most companies (and in most careers) means managing people. If you are interviewing for a supervisory position or for a job that typically leads to a management track, the interviewer will try to probe your potential in this area. So it's best to answer this question positively, even if you have never actually managed anyone on the job. Candidates with experience managing other people are considered more mature, whether or not their subordinates considered them good leaders. What's important is that they earned the confidence of their employers. If this is you, be sure to give the interviewer specific details on how many people you supervised and in what capacities these people worked. What if you haven't actually had people reporting to you? You may want to substitute the word "leadership" for "management" and talk about the clubs and other activities in which you "managed" members or volunteers or built consensus within the group. If these experiences have convinced you that you have the right stuff to be a good manager, by all means say so.

Not just management experience, but managing the same (or a slightly higher) number of people in a similarly sized and directed department or division. A positive appreciation of the varying skills needed to manage and motivate different types of employees, especially if you never actually managed anyone "on the job." No management experience for a job that requires you to manage people. (Remember, thumbs down means an answer that may make the interviewer stop and think, not necessarily one that will automatically eliminate you. If companies only hired people who have managed others, how would they ever grow their own stars?) Any negative expression of management experience. ("Yes, I managed two people at my last firm and let me tell you, they were both overpaid do-nothings!") Don't give the impression that you underestimate the requirements of management, thinking it's just an increase in prestige and money but not appreciating the pressures of increased responsibility, new skills needed, and so on. And don't appear unwilling to work to acquire them. Q: Tell me about the types of people you have trouble getting along with. What do they want to hear? This could be a land mine for a candidate who responds too quickly, answering with "pushy, abrasive people," only to find out later that the interviewer is known for being "brusque." One person I interviewed gave me what I thought was a good answer to this question: "I was discussing this problem with my boss just the other day. He told me I'm too impatient with slow performers. That the world is filled with 'C,' rather than 'A' or 'B' people, and I expect them all to be great performers. So, I guess I do have trouble with mediocre and poor workers. I don't expect to ever accept poor work, but I'm learning to be more patient."

Was he really discussing this "just the other day"? Did the conversation ever take place? Probably not, but who cares? It's a nice touch! And the answer works, too. Shouldn't any top candidate be impatient with slow performers? He even discussed what he's doing to solve his "problem." Short and sweet, but very much to the point. A general, vague answer, supplying little detail, indicates both a lack of analysis and a dearth of self-knowledge. Of course, you don't really want to answer this question—which is why it was asked. But you certainly should know it and its brethren—"What's your greatest weakness?" "Tell me about your worst boss." "Tell me about your greatest failure."—are potentially on the agenda. Variation | What types of people have trouble getting along with you? What do they want to hear? If you say "none," the interviewer will assume you're being evasive, stupid, or both. So be ready with an answer. I suggest thinking of an anecdote—a short story that softens with humor the reasons someone disliked you. A friend of mine remembered back to his first job. Just out of college, he was the first new hire in his department within a state agency in six years. Eager to succeed, he hit the ground running. From day one, he worked twice as fast as his long-term peers, who, needless to say, resented him for it. So his answer was readymade—and pretty much unverifiable—making it a near-perfect answer. Q: Who do you think are our two (or three or five) major competitors? What do they want to hear? It doesn't belong in this "group" of questions, but some interviewers like asking this question (or something like it) as early in the process as possible. It will quickly and painfully reveal the depth or shallowness of your pre-interview research. If you clearly have a handle on the company's place in the industry and can adequately, even intelligently, discuss its products, its strengths and weaknesses vs. the competition, the health of the industry, and so on, you are a serious candidate. Granted, it says absolutely nothing about your particular qualifications for the job, but if you are qualified, this display of knowledge may well be that "little extra" that separates you from other qualified (or even slightly more qualified) candidates. Although a lot of hemming, hawing, and nail-biting—along with an obvious lack of an answer—may not automatically lead to your dismissal, I would personally consider it a black mark. Variations | What's our greatest advantage over our competitors? | What's our biggest disadvantage? | Which of our new products do you think has the greatest potential for growth? | What do you think is the greatest challenge facing our company? Our industry? | Which of our products is in trouble? | What do you see as the biggest trend in our industry? Now really tell me about yourself In the world of business, "style" has little to do with how well you dress (although at some companies, and in some positions, the "right" wardrobe may be a defining element of the culture). Typically, your business style is a measure—often a subjective one, at that—of how you conduct or will conduct yourself on the job. How well do you get along with superiors? Subordinates? Peers? What's your management philosophy? Do you like to work alone or be part of a team? Interviewers will ask these types of questions to assess how you'll act and interact on the job. And interviewers will undoubtedly base at least some of their hiring decisions on their feelings about each candidate's attitude. In every case, they are assessing how the candidate's style fits in with the organizational culture, their own style, and/or the team's style. So, in general, a "thumbs up" is any answer that will convince the interviewer he or she has found a positive fit, and a "thumbs down" is an answer that reveals differences of style substantive enough to give an interviewer pause. Rather than characterizing an answer as inherently right or wrong, in other words, most interviewers are simply trying to ascertain whether you will get along with Joe or Sally or Jimmy—the other members of the company, department, or team. Following is a series of "style" questions you should probably expect to be asked somewhere along the way. Q: Are you an organized person? What do they want to hear? Even if you firmly believe that a neat desk is the sign of a sick mind, talk in detail about the organizational skills that you have developed—time management, project management, needs assessment, delegation—and how those skills have made you more effective. But don't veer too close to either extreme. No one wants to hire someone so anal-retentive that he always knows the number of paper clips in his drawer, or someone so disorganized that she'd be lucky if she remembers it's Monday. Variations | Paint me a mental picture of your current office. | Describe the top of your desk. | Tell me about the first five files in your file cabinet. | Does your smartphone help you stay organized? What apps do you use? | Do you use an online calendar? Which one?

Q: Do you manage your time well? What do they want to hear? I hope you can truthfully say yes, that you are a self-starter and almost never procrastinate. And if you can't say it truthfully, I hope you're smart enough to realize now is not the time to wail about your broken alarm clock—which is why, by the way, you were 15 minutes late for the interview, as you now remind the interviewer. Good employees are able to set goals, prioritize their tasks, and devote adequate and appropriate amounts of time to each one. In answering a rather conceptual question like this one (and what could be more conceptual than time?), try to sprinkle in specifics. Here are a few examples: "I rarely miss a deadline. When circumstances beyond my control interfere, I make up the time lost as quickly as possible." "I establish a to-do list first thing in the morning. Then I add to it—and reprioritize tasks, if necessary—as the day goes on." "I really like interacting with the people I work with. But when I need to focus on detailed tasks, I make sure to set aside time that will be free of interruptions of any kind, so I can concentrate and work more effectively." Variations | Tell me about the first 60 minutes of a typical day. | What are the first three things you do in the morning? | How often do you have to stay late to complete your work? Q: How do you handle change? What do they want to hear? Business is about change. In order to remain competitive, companies have to adapt to changes in technology, personnel,

leadership, business structure, the types of services they deliver, and even the products they produce. And their people need to change just as quickly. Choose an example of a change you faced that's resulted in something positive. Try to show that you not only accepted change and adapted to it, but flourished as a result of it, like this: "Recently, my boss decided our company needed to develop a virtual storefront on the Web. I was given the task, along with a designer, of taking the project from the research phase to operation in eight weeks. I didn't have any special expertise in the area of computers and online communications, so I have to assume I was given the task because I adapt well. "We researched the subject, examined the alternatives, and presented a plan that was accepted. Then I worked with the designer to present information in a medium neither of us had ever worked with before. In our second month online, sales were up seven percent over the same time last year." Q: How do you go about making important decisions? What do they want to hear? By now, you will have some sense of the culture of the company you're interested in working for. So shade your answer to match it. For example, if you want to work for a financial services company, you probably don't want to portray yourself as a manager who makes decisions based on "gut feeling" rather than hard data. Similarly, if you're auditioning to be an air traffic controller, it's best not to admit that you like to "sleep" on things before making up your mind. Think in terms of the interviewer's main concerns. Will you need to be analytical? Creative? Willing to call on the expertise of others? If you are aiming for a management position, you'll also want to take this opportunity to convince the interviewer that your relationship skills have made you management material—or set you on the way to achieving that goal. You might say something like this: "When I'm faced with an important decision, I ask the advice of others. I try to consider everything. But ultimately, I'm the one who decides. I guess that's why they say, 'It's lonely at the top.' The higher you go in management, the more responsibility you have and the more decisions you have to make by yourself." Although this is a nice general answer, you may run into an interviewer who decides to probe to see if the "rubber meets the road," following up with something like, "Okay, tell me about the last important decision you had to make, how you went about making it, and the results you achieved." Can you match in particulars the nice general answer given above? Or do you inadvertently show you do things completely differently (better or worse) than you just said you did? Q: Do you work well under pressure? What do they want to hear? Naturally, everyone will say yes to this question. However, it will be best to provide examples that support your claim to being the Second Coming of Cool Hand Luke. Be sure to choose anecdotes that don't imply that the pressure you've faced has resulted from your own procrastination or failure to anticipate problems. Variation | Tell me about a time pressure led you to indecision, a poor decision, or a mistake. What would you have done differently? Have you found yourself in a similar situation since? What did you do? The questioning pattern I am suggesting you prepare for throughout this book should be apparent by now: Good interviewers

will probe, probe, then probe some more. Why? Because they figure you can only rehearse so many generalizations and remember a limited number of little white lies, so the more detailed their questions, the more likely you will inadvertently reveal any misrepresentations, exaggerations, or omissions. Q: Do you anticipate problems well or merely react to them? What do they want to hear? All managers panic from time to time. The best learn to protect themselves by anticipating problems that might lie around the bend. For example, one sales manager I know had his staff provide reports on all positive—and negative—budget variances on a weekly basis. By sharing this valuable information with his boss and also with the manufacturing, distribution, and marketing arms of the company, he helped improve product turnover and boost flagging sales. This kind of story is terrific fodder for successful interviews and the kind of example you should be trying to provide. Q: Are you a risk-taker or do you prefer to play it safe? What do they want to hear? In most cases, the ideal candidate will be a mixture of both. Interviewers who ask this question are probing for intimations of innovation and creativity. Are you the shepherd or just one of the flock? But they also want to find out whether you might turn into a "loose cannon" that will ignore company policies and be all too ready to lead a fatal cavalry charge. Again, this is a highly (company) cultural question. The interviewer might personally prefer Stonewall Jackson, CEO, to be leading his troops into battle, but probably wouldn't want him to be controller. Variations | Tell me about the last time you took a risk. Was it the right decision? What would you have done differently? | Tell me about a time you played it safe. Did you miss an opportunity or avoid a debacle?

Q: If you could start your career over again, what would you do differently? What do they want to hear? Interviewers use hypothetical questions to get candidates to think on their feet. They expect you to "know your lines" when it comes to the facts about your career and education. But how will you react when you have to ignore the script and ad lib? Unless you're attempting a complete change of career, you must convince the interviewer that you wouldn't change a thing. You love your career and, given the chance, you'd do it all over again. Feel free to quote Paul Anka (via Sinatra): "Regrets? I've had a few. But all in all, too few to mention." In this case, however, watch which ones you do mention and make sure you position them in a way that shows what you've learned. Did you leave your first job because you were too impatient for a promotion, only to realize you hadn't learned all you could have? Did you miss the opportunity to specialize in some area or develop a particular expertise that you should have? "My only regret is that I didn't go in this direction sooner. I started my career in editorial, and I enjoyed that. But once I got into marketing, I found I really loved it. Now, I can't wait to get to work every day." "I wish I had never gotten into magazine publishing in the first place. But now I guess I'm stuck. And to think, I could have been editing garden books for FernMoor Press..." Variations | What was the biggest mistake you ever made when choosing a job? | How important a factor has money been in your career choices?

Q: Do you prefer to work by yourself or with others? What do they want to hear? Again, the position you're interviewing for will dictate how you should shape your answer. For example, if you're interviewing for a job as an on-the-road sales rep—who may develop an unhealthy crush on her rental car but will otherwise interact solely with customers, wait staff, and hotel employees—you won't want to admit that you thrive on your relationships with coworkers and can't imagine working without a lot of interaction. Even if you do like the interaction at work, don't try to paint your environment as a bed of roses without any thorns. You know the old saying: "You can choose your friends, but you can't choose your relatives." That goes for coworkers, too. Every job situation forces us to get along with people we might not choose to socialize with. But we must get along with them and, quite often, for long stretches of time and under difficult circumstances. Acknowledging this reality is essential. Talk about how you've managed to get along with a variety of other people. Once I was interviewing candidates for a position managing a production department with 16 employees. Production departments in publishing companies are filled with some of the quirkiest people you'll ever come across, so I had to gauge the interpersonal skills of each applicant very carefully. After I'd asked one candidate a couple of questions about his management and communication skills, he gave me a steady look and said: "Look, you know and I know it's not always easy to manage artists and proofreaders. I do my best to convince them of the importance of deadlines and let them know what it costs us when we miss them. I also point out how unfair it is to others in the department, and to the entire operation, when things are held up unnecessarily.

"I usually find some way to get along with all of the people in the department, some way to convince them that timeliness and accuracy are absolute musts. It's not always easy. But a lot of times it's fun. When we are rushed because another department is late, I use this as an object lesson. The most important thing is to distribute the work fairly and let everyone know that you expect them to do their share." Needless to say, this "right-on" answer won the job. Variations | How do you get along with your superior(s)? With your coworkers? With your subordinates? | How much time per week do you spend working alone? Do you think it should be more? Less? | Do you enjoy doing individual research? | Do you tend to procrastinate when left alone? What do they want to hear? The answers to these questions should, first of all, bear some relation to the answers to earlier questions about people with whom you have had trouble or who have had trouble getting along with you. But this is, yet again, a highly cultural question, and one for which the requirements of the job define the "rightness" of any answer. If you thrive working alone but the interviewer is seeking someone who will always be part of a team, the dichotomy will be obvious. Q: How do you generally handle conflict? What do they want to hear? "I really don't get angry with other people very often. I'm usually able to work things out or anticipate problems before they occur. When conflicts can't be avoided, I don't back down. But I certainly do try to be reasonable."

Or: "I've had confrontations with coworkers who weren't holding up their end of a job. I feel that employees owe it to their bosses, customers, and coworkers to do their jobs properly." Q: How do you behave when you have a problem with a coworker? What do they want to hear? "I had to work with a designer who just refused to listen to any of my suggestions. He would answer me in monosyllables and then drag his feet before doing anything I requested. Finally, I said, 'Look, we're both professionals. Neither of us has the right answer all the time. I have noticed that you don't really like my suggestions. But rather than resist implementing them, why don't we just discuss what you don't like?' "That worked like a charm. In fact, we eventually became friends." Variations | Tell me about the last time you lost your temper. | How often do you get angry? | How do you deal with difficult people? | Tell me about the last time you disagreed with your boss. A coworker. A subordinate. What did you do and what was the result? Q: How do you motivate people? What do they want to hear? A good answer will note how it "depends on the person," then offer one or two concrete examples. A poor candidate will imply that all people are motivated by the same thing or can be motivated with the same approach, a kind of "one-size-fits-all" philosophy. A savvy interviewer will use this as a follow-up question to "What is your management philosophy?"

Tips for Handling Questions About Work q Be honest. But play up your strengths and whitewash your weaknesses. If you have to talk about negative experiences, point out what you learned from them and why you wouldn't make the same mistakes again. q Introduce only positives. Don't give away information that could come back to haunt you. q Strike a balance between portraying yourself as a "company man or woman" and a "loose cannon." Screening interviewers and hiring managers are often attracted to risk-takers. But they also put a lot of stock in playing by the rules. Your pre-interview research should clarify which road to take. If in doubt, choose neither— settle for a balanced reply. q Use specific work situations to substantiate your claims. If you sense the interview drifting into subjectivity, regain the upper hand by citing concrete examples from your past experience. Don't just say you're organized. Tell how you organized a complex project from beginning to end. Remember, insofar as possible, you want the interviewer basing his or her decision on the facts—your strengths, qualifications, and accomplishments—not some subjective evaluation of "chemistry." q Choose your words carefully. Make sure that you are indeed answering questions and not suggesting other areas the interviewer hadn't thought to explore. For example, I suggest, "I'm looking for greater challenges," rather than, "The boss didn't give me enough to do." Do you really want to travel down that road?

Sometimes you just can't win Some people have always had a job—in fact, a lot of jobs. And companies are especially cautious about hiring people who have changed jobs repeatedly. Curiously enough, however, many are equally cautious about hiring people who have never moved. If either of these situations describes your particular job history, here's how to handle it. Q: You've changed jobs quite frequently. How do we know you'll stick around? What do they want to hear? The hiring process is expensive for companies and time-consuming for managers. Job-hoppers only serve to make it a more frequent process. So, in framing your reply, convince the interviewer you have staying power by painting the position on offer as your career's "Promised Land." Take one of these two approaches: Confess that you had some difficulty defining your career goals at first, but now you are quite sure of your direction. Convince the interviewer that you left previous positions only after you realized that moving on was the only way to increase your responsibilities and broaden your experience. Be sure to emphasize the fact that you would like nothing better than to stay and grow with a company. Here's an example to study if you have to explain your own job-hopping history: Sherri had four jobs in the first six years after college graduation. Her clever reply to an interviewer's skepticism about her staying power combines both techniques: "All through college, I was convinced that I wanted to be a programmer. But after a few months in my first job, I found that I was unhappy. Naturally, I blamed the company and the job. So when an opportunity opened up at Lakeside Bank, I grabbed it. But not long after the initial euphoria wore off, I was unhappy again. "By this time I'd noticed that I really did enjoy the part of my job that dealt with applications. So when I heard about the job in end-user computing at SafeInvest, I went for it. I learned a lot there, until I hit a 'glass ceiling.' It was a small firm, so there was no place for me to grow. "I was recruited for the applications position at Deep Pockets Bank, and I got the job because of some of the innovations I'd developed at SI. The work has been terrific. But once again, I find that I'm a one-person department. "This position offers the opportunity to manage a department and interact with programmers and applications specialists on the cutting edge of technology. Throughout my career, the one thing that has remained constant is my love of learning. This job would give me the chance to learn so much." Variation | You've been with your current employer for only a short amount of time. Is this an indication that you'll be moving around a lot throughout your career? Q: You've been with the same organization for years. Won't you have a tough time getting used to a different culture and structure? What do they want to hear? This is the corollary of the previous question. Here's what the interviewer is doing to you: If you've moved around, she questions your staying power. If you stuck with a single company, she questions your initiative. It seems like a lose-lose situation for you. Here's how to fight back: During your tenure with your current company, you've probably worked for more than one boss. You may even have supervised many different types of people in various departments. Certainly you've teamed up with a variety of coworkers. And from inside this one organization, you've had a chance to observe a wide variety of other organizations—competitors, vendors, customers, and so on. You're both flexible and loyal, which can prove a valuable combination. By the time you've been asked introductory questions, questions about high school and college experiences, and these preliminary "on-the-job" questions, you should certainly have an idea of whether you are still a viable candidate. And if you are, you can expect even more questions. (If you are not, you can expect to be led politely to the door any time now.) If the interviewer is still unsure, it's time for her to ask even more detailed questions. She's invited you to paint her a picture. Okay, Rembrandt, what else do you have to offer her?

7

Questions About Core Competencies

Now that the generalities have been covered—pesky things such as motivation and your basic on-the-job attitude—good interviewers will try to glean even more particular information on your past performance. Take heart—if you've made it this far, you're still a viable candidate! Q: Tell me about the last time you: Ö Made a mistake. Ö Made a good decision. Ö Made a poor decision. Ö Fired someone. Ö Hired someone. Ö Delegated an important assignment. Ö Led a team. Ö Successfully completed a complex project. Ö Failed to complete a project on time. Ö Learned a new skill. Ö Developed a new expertise. Ö Found a unique solution to a problem. Ö Found a creative solution to a problem. Ö Found a cost-effective solution to a problem.

Ö Rallied your team. Ö Motivated a troubled employee. Ö Aimed too high. Ö Aimed too low. Ö Made (or lost) a great sale. Ö Saved the company money. Ö Cost the company money. Ö Went over budget. Ö Exceeded your own expectations. Ö Exceeded your boss's expectations. Ö Fell short of your boss's expectations. Ö Had to think on your feet. Ö Had to make an unpopular decision. Ö Had to implement an unpopular decision. Ö Dealt with a difficult boss. Ö Dealt with a difficult customer. Ö Dealt with a difficult coworker. Ö Dealt with a difficult subordinate. Ö Were frustrated at work. Ö Were angry at work. Ö Were stressed at work. Ö Delivered a speech or major presentation. Ö Questioned your boss's decision. Ö Convinced your boss to change his decision. Ö Went over your boss's head. Ö Lost a battle but won the war. What do they want to hear? As I briefly discussed in Chapter 1, these are examples of competency-based interview questions. What are they trying to discover? According to Robin Kessler's Competency-based Interviews, there are three general groups of competencies—those dealing with people, with business, and with self-management. Competencies dealing with people include: Ö Establishing focus Ö Providing motivational support Ö Fostering teamwork Ö Empowering others Ö Managing change Ö Developing others Ö Managing performance Ö Attention to communication Ö Oral communication Ö Written communication Ö Persuasive communication Ö Interpersonal awareness Ö Influencing others Ö Building collaborative relationships Ö Customer orientation Competencies dealing with business include: Ö Diagnostic information gathering Ö Analytical thinking Ö Forward thinking Ö Conceptual thinking Ö Strategic thinking Ö Technical expertise Ö Initiative Ö Entrepreneurial orientation Ö Fostering innovation Ö Results orientation Ö Thoroughness Ö Decisiveness Finally, self-management competencies include: Ö Self-confidence Ö Stress management Ö Personal credibility Ö Flexibility All such questions seem open-ended, like "Tell me about yourself," encouraging you to talk, but these clearly require focused, specific answers. Based on your initial answer, follow-up questions will seek even greater detail: "Okay, I understand how the lack of divisional coordination led to the budget shortfall. And you have clearly taken responsibility for your part in the miscommunication. But what did you do to change procedures to ensure it didn't happen again? And, by the way, did it happen again?" Expect a seasoned interviewer to keep probing and asking for more specifics, more examples, who said what, who did what, what were the results, what would you do differently now, what do you need to change to do better in the future, what have you changed, and so on. The more detailed and clear-cut the job description, the more likely the interviewer has identified the particular competencies required to succeed at it...and the more questions will focus on those specific requirements. A specific answer to a specific question, the more detailed the better. An answer to any of the above questions that has a beginning, middle, and end, much like a good story: Here's what happened, here's what I did, here's what I learned. Some of the questions require job-related answers; others may allow for examples chosen from outside activities, perhaps volunteer work or any part of one's personal life. A savvy candidate will "mix and match" stories and examples to convince an interviewer she is well-rounded and actually has a life after 5 p.m. Take appropriate credit for an accomplishment (reducing costs, increasing revenues, a creative solution, a tough sale) but be fair and honest enough to put your own contribution within the context of what your team/organization/boss/assistants did...and try to appear to be bending over backward to do so. Most interviewers will favor a candidate who has been around long enough to make good and bad decisions, good and bad hires, good and bad choices. The breadth of your exposure to the basic tenets of business is more important to me, anyway, than the extent of your experience. Avoid giving the impression you're a "hardworking, self-starting, high-energy" Mr. Generalization who can't furnish an interviewer with too many examples of your wonderfulness, no matter how many questions she tosses you. Most interviewers will be suspicious of someone with years of experience in the same job that seems to have enjoyed little exposure to the normal day-to-day vagaries of the world. You hired someone once and they were fine. Never fired anyone. Can't remember the last time you actually had to make a major decision. No matter how talented you are (or think you are), avoid claiming to have been CEO/COO/CFO/creative star/sales guru—all at the same time. Even if you are a prodigy who would give Mozart pause, you should be savvy enough not to take credit for every success your company achieved in the last decade (especially if you've only been there three years). I always found it interesting, for example, that seven different independent publicists approached me at a trade show and that every single one of them claimed—in their literature and even on their business cards—to be totally responsible for the success of the book, Chicken Soup for the Soul. While I'm not sure every one of them had even worked on the book, clearly not every one of them was singularly in charge of the publicity plan! Q: What do you do when you're having trouble... Ö Solving a problem? Ö With a subordinate? Ö With a boss? Ö With your job? Q: What do you do when... Ö Things are slow? Ö Things are hectic? Ö You're burned out? Ö You have multiple priorities (family/work/school, etc.)? What do they want to hear? These questions are just further attempts to figure out how you think and act in reality. You may well have been asked about problems with a boss, coworkers, or subordinates 10, 20, or 30 minutes before, so be careful—a good interviewer may be trying to trip you up by homing in on the same issue from a different direction. The style of question framed along the lines of "What do you do when..." is very different from "Do you have a problem with ?" Q: What skills do you most need to acquire or develop to advance your career? What do they want to hear? You should claim to be developing a skill in line with the job for which you're interviewing, otherwise why are you talking about it? "Well, I really need to grip my tennis racquet more firmly at the net. My stroke is just all wrong." Let me rephrase this question: Q: What do your supervisors tend to criticize most about your performance? What do they want to hear? This is another way of framing a series of questions you've probably already been asked: What's your greatest weakness? What was your greatest failure? What would your supervisor say about you? Asking what amounts to the same question three or four different ways gives a seasoned interviewer the ability to look for the inconsistencies that you might well reveal. You should certainly assume your references will be checked—and your current supervisor contacted—so your answer better match what your supervisor says. Consider discussing an evaluation from an earlier job, switching to what you did about it, and claiming that your current supervisor would, therefore, not consider it a problem any longer. This is a really beautiful answer because it's possible that the interviewer can't really check the initial evaluation, which makes the rest of the scenario moot—but it works for you! Just remember: A good interviewer will find a way to get around this elegant subterfuge: "Was there anything your current supervisor criticized you for in your last performance evaluation?" or "What specific areas did your current supervisor's last evaluation indicate you needed to work on?" Never cite a personal quality that might (or convince the interviewer that it might) hamper your job performance, such as procrastination, laziness, lack of concentration, a hot temper or tardiness. Most interviewers probably will be suspicious if you claim never to have received a poor evaluation. While not necessarily untrue— there are companies and bosses that fail to do systematic evaluations or fail to take them very seriously—it will probably just lead you to these follow-up questions: "Tell me about the last time your boss criticized you. What for? What was your response? What have you done to fix/solve/change what he criticized?" I would find it highly suspect for any candidate to claim they have never been called on the carpet for anything. Q: Did you inaugurate new procedures (systems, policies, etc.) in your previous position? Tell me about them. What do they want to hear? Of course! You had some very good solutions you'd be happy to share with the interviewer. Regrettably, however, some (or none?) could be implemented because of circumstances beyond your control. You don't have to be a divisional president or department head to answer this question. An administrative assistant may have creatively and by his or her own volition instituted a new filing system or a better way to delegate departmental correspondence, or simply utilized technology to improve a mundane task, like keeping the boss's calendar. The interviewer is seeking industriousness, creativity, and someone who clearly cares about the organization and its success. So this is the time to bring up those facts and figures we talked about earlier. Describe the changes or improvements you were responsible for making and identify how they helped the company, in terms of increased profits, cost savings or improved production. Variation | Was there anything your company (or department or team) could have done to be more successful? Here's a perfectly acceptable answer: "Sure, we could have expanded our product line, perhaps even doubled it, to take advantage of our superior distribution. But we just didn't have the capital and couldn't get the financing." Q: Have you been in charge of budgeting, approving expenses, and monitoring departmental progress against financial goals? Are you very qualified in this area? What do they want to hear? Again, financial responsibility signals an employer's faith in you. If you haven't had many—or any—fiscal duties, admit it. But as always, nothing is stopping you from being creative in the way you frame your reply. Here's an example: "Well, I've never actually run a department, but I've had to set and meet budgetary goals for several projects I've worked on. In fact, I did this so often that I took a class to learn how to set up and use Microsoft Excel spreadsheets." If you've had broader responsibilities, talk about your approval authority. What is the largest expenditure you could sign off on? Let the interviewer know, in round numbers, the income and expenses of the departments you've supervised. Be careful. This question is also designed to trap you if you lied in the previous question. "So, Ron, you managed 14 people but had no financial responsibilities at all? Hmmm..." If you answer this question positively, expect more probing: "In your experience, what are the most common obstacles you've faced when completing assignments or projects on time and on budget? Give me one or two examples of how you dealt with them." Q: Have you ever fired anyone? Why? What do they want to hear? Even if you had good reason, you know that firing someone is never pleasant. Say so, and provide a "sanitized" (and brief!) version of the events to the interviewer. Remember, you don't want to seem like a negative person, one who might disrupt an entire department, nor appear too empathetic. You should express a modicum of sympathy for the person (people) who got the axe (you clearly didn't relish your role), an understanding that sometimes people have to be fired (business is business), and a readiness to do it appropriately, professionally, and compassionately, when required. Let's say you fired someone for not meeting productivity goals. You might be thinking, "Boy, I'm glad I got rid of that bum. He was nothing but a wimp and whiner who never did a good day's work in all the time he was on the job." Go ahead and think that. But when you open your mouth, say something like this: "Yes, I fired someone who continually fell short of his productivity goals. His shortcomings were documented and discussed with him over a period of months. But in that time, he failed to show any real improvement. I had no choice. As a supervisor, I want everyone in my department to work out. Let's face it, though, not everyone is equally dedicated to his or her job." If you haven't actually fired anyone, here is one way to respond: "I've never actually fired anyone myself, but it was the policy at my company that no hirings or firings should be unilateral. I was asked on two occasions to give my opinion about someone else's performance. It's never easy to be honest about a coworker's shortcomings. But I felt I had to do what was best for the department and fair to everyone else in it." Q: Have you ever hired anyone? Why did you choose them? What do they want to hear? If you have hired one or more people during your career, your answer might go something like this: "Yes, I have hired people. I have also decided whether some internal applicants were right for jobs in my department. The first time I hired someone, I concentrated on checking off all the right qualifications. I just went down a checklist.

"Since then, I've learned that some candidates who became excellent workers didn't necessarily have every qualification on that checklist. They more than made up for what they lacked in the beginning with enthusiasm and a willingness to work with others." What if you've never hired anyone? Show the interviewer you appreciate that he or she is trying to evaluate both your management potential and people skills, and try something like this: "Not really. But on several occasions I was asked to speak to prospective applicants and offer my opinion. Of course, in those cases, I was trying to determine whether that person would be a team player and if he or she would get along with the other people in the department." Let's take it from the top If you're seeking an executive-level position, most of the previous questions in this book are just as pertinent as if you were interviewing to be a receptionist (although the interviewer would expect a different level of answer). Here are a few questions you can expect if you are a potential CEO, CFO, CIO, or executive vice president: Q: Describe your management philosophy. What do they want to hear? Most companies want someone who can demonstrate a desire and ability to delegate, teach. and distribute work—and credit— fairly (unless, of course, the interviewer is an autocratic jerk seeking a mirror image). In general, you probably want to come across as neither a dictator nor a pushover. Successful candidates will convey that they have the ability to succeed should opportunity present itself. But they should avoid giving the impression that they're fire-breathing workaholics ready to succeed no matter what (or whom) the cost.

"More than anything else, I think that management is getting things done through other people. The manager's job is to provide the resources and environment in which people can work effectively. I try to do this by creating teams, judging people solely on the basis of their performance, distributing work fairly, and empowering workers, to the extent possible, to make their own decisions. I've found that this breeds loyalty and inspires hard work." These are wishy-washy answers I've actually heard during interviews: "I try to get people to like me, and then they really work hard for me." "I guess you could say I'm a real people person." "I just kind of go with the flow and see what happens." Q: What's the most difficult part of being a manager or executive? Q: Tell me about the last situation in which you were directed to overhaul a problem unit/department/division/company. What were you confronted with, what did you do, what kind of culture did you attempt to create? Q: How many people did you hire and fire? Q: What goals did you establish? Q: How long was your outlook, and what were the results? What do they want to hear? Every question is designed to get a handle on your management philosophy and gauge your abilities to conceptualize on a general basis and implement on a specific one: to foster loyalty, unity, and shared goals; to create and produce under pressure; to stay within budget and/or produce over budget; and so on.

Needless to say, very specific examples that detail the problems you've faced, the actions you took and the results you achieved, are called for. Variations | What kinds of decisions are difficult for you to make? | How do you go about making a decision? | How do you decide what tasks to delegate and to whom? | Tell me about the last responsibility you delegated that went wrong. | What was the worst decision you ever made? | How much feedback do you want from your subordinates? | Tell me about the last decision you made that your subordinates disagreed with. | Tell me about the last decision you made that your boss disagreed with. Q: How do you "stay in the loop"? What do they want to hear? There are many ways to get the information an interviewer is seeking with this question. Here are some variations: Ö How many meetings do you schedule and/or attend per week? Per month? Ö Do you believe in "Management by Walking Around"? Ö Do you spend a lot of time in your subordinates' offices asking questions or do you prefer to wait for them to come to you with problems? Ö Tell me about the last time you skipped a meeting. Why didn't you attend? Ö What regular communications do you expect from your employees?

All of the above are much more specific than "Explain your management philosophy," a question an experienced interviewee can wiggle through with a couple of business-guru quotes. The more senior your current position—and the more "executive" the position for which you're applying—the more likely these types of questions will be asked. And the more important the answers to them will be. Q: How do you deal with subordinates who are becoming part of the problem rather than part of the solution? What do they want to hear? This has been asked previously in other forms. The interviewer is trying to separate the real leaders from the "managers with a title" and ascertain whether your particular style will mesh with that of the organization. A matter of ethics Q: Tell me about your personal code of ethics? Are you an ethical person? What is your moral code? I would seek to emphasize one's honesty, loyalty, and integrity, all attributes any company should value and welcome. If your personal sense of ethics or morals is based on your religious upbringing or faith, I would not feel it necessary (or advisable) to trumpet that fact. As we will see in Chapter 10, the interviewer has no right to ask about your religion, so why raise the issue yourself? And if you are willing to do just about anything to get ahead and barely know the difference between right and wrong? Please don't confess your lack of integrity to the interviewer...or schedule an interview at my company. Variations | Tell me about the last time you did something inconsistent with your values or ethics.

| Have you ever had to "bend the rules" to do your job? | Tell me about the last time you uncovered or learned about a coworker's unethical behavior. What did you do? | What would you do if you learned this company was doing something you thought was wrong? Q: Would you lie for your company? Sorry, no. That certainly doesn't mean you won't be loyal and willing to go the extra mile, but you will not compromise your own ethics. Q: A colleague told you she is looking for a job but asked you to keep her confidence. What would you say if your boss asked you point-blank about it? Well, you are not a snitch and you can certainly keep a secret, but you have to demonstrate that your loyalty to the company trumps your loyalty to a colleague, subordinate, or friend. Can you think of any (equally hypothetical) way to protect that person's confidence without lying to your

boss? Finding such a solution would certainly highlight your diplomatic skills. Variations | Would you lie to cover up a mistake or ethical violation by your boss (colleague, subordinate, team member)? | When is it okay to break a confidence? | When is it okay to reveal another's secret? Can you keep a secret and respect confidentiality? Companies protecting valuable patents, product recipes, and other corporate secrets are now assailed daily by computer hackers. A loss of confidential information to a competitor could be devastating. Can they trust you to put the company first? Are you part of the solution or another potential leaker or whistleblower they have to worry about?

Be positive about your reasons for leaving your current job (or any previous jobs, for that matter). The key word to remember is "more." You want more responsibility, more challenges, more opportunity, and finally (but don't play this up, except as a natural consequence of the previous "mores"), more money. q If you've been fired, stress what you learned from the experience. Be as positive as you can be. q Quantify the confidence other employers have placed in you. Do this by stressing specific facts, figures, and measurable accomplishments. Mention the number of employees you've supervised, the amount of money you controlled, the earnings that your department achieved under your management. q Never speak badly of past supervisors or employers. It's the biggest negative of all, and you're highlighting nothing but the positive, right? q Make the job you're interviewing for your chief objective. Frame your answers so that you let the interviewer know that you see this job as a means to achieving your ultimate career objectives. Be careful not to make it sound like either a stepping stone or a safe haven.

8

Questions About Your Current (or Last) Job

Whether you have been working for 20 years or 20 days, you will probably face a lot of questions about your current or last job. Even if it boasted the shortest tenure. Even if a previous job lasted years and your current one just months. Why? Because the interviewer wants to know what you can do for him or her right now—and the most current job offers the best available proof. Q: Why are you thinking of leaving your current job? What do they want to hear? Obviously, no one wants to leave a job with which they are completely content (although some people routinely interview to keep "in practice" or explore other opportunities in their area or industry). But the last thing you want to do is appear negative or, worse, speak ill of your current employer. (If you do so, your interviewer will assume that if you're hired, you will soon be characterizing him and/or his company in the same disparaging terms.) So handle your discontent (if that's what led you here) very gingerly. The less contented you are, the more careful you should be in talking about it. It will do you absolutely no good to confess to the interviewer that you lie awake most nights fantasizing about putting a contract out on your current boss. Instead, use what management consultants call "visioning": Imagine the ideal next step in your career, then act as though you are interviewing for that position. Here's what I mean. Let's say you are interested in assuming more financial management responsibilities. You might tell the interviewer: "There is a great deal I enjoy about my current job. But my potential for growth in this area is limited at Closely Held, Inc., because of the size of the company and the fact that expansion isn't part of its current strategic plan." Unless you've been fired or laid off, you should make it clear that you are sitting in front of the interviewer only because you seek more responsibility, a bigger challenge, or better opportunities for growth (even more money), not because you are desperate to put some distance between yourself and your current job situation. Emphasize your desire to move "up" rather than just to move "out." Avoid any personal and/or negative comments about coworkers, supervisors, or your current (last) company's policies. The introduction of any negative, no matter how horrible your current job situation. (In fact, the more obviously horrible your job, the more points you will score with many interviewers for creating an impression of relative contentment.) A willingness to make a lateral move or even take a demotion just to leave your current company. Unless you are moving into an entirely new area or field, such a willingness to move out rather than up would give me pause. What are you hiding? Is this just a last-ditch effort to get out before you are shoved out? And what does such a willingness say about your ability to tough it out until the right situation comes along? Is my company just a calmer sea in which to tread water until the right freighter passes by?

Variations | What's hindering your progress at your present firm? | Is this the first time you've thought about leaving? What made you stay before? | If the situation is so dire, why haven't you already given notice? Q: Where does your boss think you are now? What do they want to hear? Although you may have been given notice or laid off and, therefore, be interviewing with the full knowledge of your boss, it's more likely you're still employed. So under no circumstances mutter something like, "He thinks I'm interviewing with you so I can leave that hellhole behind. By the way, he'll be calling you tomorrow to find a job himself." You should attempt to schedule interviews during lunch hour, after work, or on a personal or vacation day. I personally don't like to hear that a candidate has taken a sick day to talk with me. It's a white lie, but a lie nevertheless. The truth, whatever it is. Many interviewers will give you points for demonstrating your sense of responsibility to your current job by scheduling a breakfast interview or one during a lunch hour or after hours. If you have blatantly lied or indicate through body language that the question makes you uncomfortable (implying that you lied). If your answer demonstrates little or no loyalty to the company that's still paying the bills, whether that organization is enlightened or despotic. Q: Are you still employed at the last firm listed on your resume? What do they want to hear? You probably know the adage that it's always easier to find a job when you already have one. Well, it's true, because many interviewers believe that an employed person is somehow "better" than an unemployed one, even if the latter is more qualified. Being laid off is perceived by many interviewers as a sign of weakness. I even heard one experienced executive recruiter say, "Oh, if she was laid off, there must be something wrong with her. Companies don't ever let really good employees go!" Would that it were true! But the fact is that massive layoffs can and do still occur. And many hardworking, loyal individuals who contributed greatly to their companies—and could be significant assets to a new one— have to admit they've been laid off. Personally, I am firmly convinced that there is no shame in this status and give a laid-off candidate the same consideration I do anyone else. I would not assume all interviewers are as enlightened. What if you were fired? Come clean quickly and smoothly to turn this potential negative into a positive. Let's consider the case of Nick. A hotel sales manager, he was unfortunate enough to work for a petty tyrant who made a practice of taking Nick and his coworkers to task often, publicly and mercilessly. One day, Nick finally had it. He blew up at his boss—and was fired on the spot. Later on, he was asked about his employment status in an interview for another hotel sales job. He answered bluntly, "I was fired." When the stunned interviewer asked to hear more, Nick explained: "My boss and I just didn't get along, and I have to admit I didn't handle the situation well. I certainly understand the importance of call reports and log sheets and other sales-management controls. I guess I interpreted some of Joe's quick demands for these things as a lack of trust, and I shouldn't have. I've learned my lesson." Talk less about why you were terminated and more about what you've learned from the experience. If you were laid off, or, as the British quaintly say, "made redundant," you shouldn't be expected to apologize. You might say something like, "Yes, I was one of 16 people laid off when sales took a slide." (This is an easy way out—presuming you were not a member, or head, of the sales department!) As always, the introduction of any negative. ("Yeah, I was fired because I'm not as young as I used to be. Wait until they see what my old lawyer has to say about age discrimination. I'll make them pay through the nose!") Being fired for cause, especially if you refuse to admit responsibility or detail what steps have been taken to correct the problem. Celebrity felons like Mike Tyson may get two or three or umpteen chances to make millions even after serving time, but most interviewers get a bit antsy about hiring someone who was fired for stealing, drinking on the job, hitting their boss, or some equally charming offense. Q: Describe the way your department is organized. Also, what is the title of the person to whom you report? What are his or her exact responsibilities? What do they want to hear? Did you hear that? If you've been vastly exaggerating the duties and responsibilities of your current position, that sound you heard was the door that just closed...behind you...on your way out of the interview. This question is designed to clarify what you really do—how can you be doing "X" if you said that's your boss's main function?—and set up a series of follow-up questions about why you exaggerated (presuming the interviewer doesn't just say "thank you" then and there). Don't be surprised if you are asked to draw an organizational chart of your company or department. Duties and responsibilities that match those claimed on your resume. Duties and responsibilities commensurate with the job at hand. An answer that ties in with your answers to previous questions about work experience. The more detailed these answers, the easier it will be for an interviewer to catch any inconsistencies (at which point he or she will return to those previous answers and ask why the current one doesn't seem to mesh with them). A clearly presented explanation of how your department, division, or company is set up, which tends to at least show consistency with your resume and implies that you have really done what you said you have (although a really good interviewer will take detailed notes so he or she can check each particular with your supervisor when calling for a reference). A hazy, vague explanation that indicates you may be making it all up as you go along. Glaring inconsistencies with your resume or previous answers. Failure to include a key responsibility or job duty that was previously proclaimed, especially if it's one that is important to the new job. An organizational plan that doesn't make sense to the interviewer. (The more experience someone has at different companies, the more likely she will have been exposed to different structures and management styles, and the more confident she will feel that a structure that seems top heavy or one that gives lower-level staff members an extraordinary amount of freedom doesn't "feel right.")

Q: Tell me about your typical day at your current (last) job. How much time do you spend on the phone? In meetings? In one-on-one chats? Working by yourself? Working with your team (or others)? What do they want to hear? Again, they are looking for the detail that will "prove" some of the earlier general statements you made (about responsibilities, duties, even favorite aspects of your job) or show that those statements were disingenuous or perhaps somewhat excessive. Variations | On a typical day, tell me what you do in the first and last hour at work. When do you arrive and leave? | Tell me what specific responsibilities you currently delegate. Are you delegating too many or too few tasks? Why? What's stopping you from changing it? | How many hours per week do you have to work to fulfill your responsibilities at work? | What's the most important part of your current job to you? To your firm? Q: How long have you been looking for a job? What do they want to hear? Unless you've been fired or laid off, your answer should always be that you've just started looking. If you think the interviewer has some way of finding out that you've been looking for a while (perhaps you've come to him through a recruiter who knows your history), be prepared to explain why you haven't received or accepted any offers. Rightly or wrongly, many interviewers presume that the longer you've been "out there," the less desirable you are to hire. Personally, I disagree. If someone's been looking for a month or two or three, are they inherently less desirable than a newly minted ex-employee who's still wearing his company T-shirt under his suit? It's unrealistic to expect that everyone who wants a job can find one right away. It's even less realistic not to assume that the most qualified candidates might well be picky and simply be ensuring a proper fit with the right company before plunging back into the corporate seas. Nevertheless, be prepared to deal with those interviewers less understanding than I. Variations | How's your job search going? | How optimistic are you about getting a job? Q: What other companies have you interviewed with? This is a not-so-veiled way to see whether you are being consistent—you just declared this company is the end-all and be-all of your search, but all the other companies with which you've interviewed are in entirely different industries, some in entirely different locations. What is the interviewer to believe? How serious are you? Variations | Have you interviewed with any of our competitors? | Why haven't you gotten interviews with more companies? | Why have you interviewed with so many companies? | Why did you interview with them? Q: Why haven't you received any offers so far? What do they want to hear? You're just as choosy about finding the right job as the interviewer is about hiring the right candidate. Don't whine or show that the search is upsetting you. If you've already fielded an offer or two, you might say: "I have had an offer. But the situation was not right for me. I'm especially glad that I didn't accept, because I now have a shot at landing this position." It's important to tell the truth, however, because the interviewer's next logical question may be: Q: Who made you an offer? For what type of position? At what salary? What do they want to hear? If you've already lied, you're in hot water now! Some interviewers will consider any admission of lying in these circumstances your "voluntary" offer to end the interview. Many interviewers know a great deal about their competitors and which positions they're trying to fill. If you did the smart thing and told the truth, supply the name of the company. He or she may already be aware of your visit there. It's important to stress that the position you turned down was very similar to the one you're applying for now. After all, if the job you are currently interviewing for is perfect for you— as you've undoubtedly already told the interviewer three or four times—why would you be interested in a very different position at the other company? Q: If you don't leave your current job, what will happen there? How far do you expect to advance? What do they want to hear? Is desperation driving you away from your current job, so that you'll say or do anything to get this one? This doesn't exactly make you a prime candidate to most interviewers. Why should he or she save you? Even if you'd rather hawk peanuts at the circus than stay another month at ABC Widget, convince the interviewer that you're the type of employee who is capable of making the most of any situation—even an employment situation you've characterized as undesirable. You could say: "Naturally I'm interested in this job and have been thinking about leaving ABC. However, my supervisors think highly of me, and I expect that one day other situations will open up for me at the company. I'm one of ABC's top salespeople. I have seen other people performing at similar levels advance to management positions. But I'm looking for that increased responsibility right now." However you really feel about your current job, it's always best to conduct your part of the interview as if you are in the driver's seat, just cruising along happily until you see that changing lanes would improve your career. You certainly aren't interested in getting off at the next exit, no matter where it leads! Begin your answers with the phrase, "Well, assuming I'm not the successful candidate for this position...." Without too much ego, let the interviewer know that you're taking your time. You're interested in choosing a job that's right for you. If you can claim (or do claim) that you will still advance and be given more responsibility, but perhaps at too slow a pace or without adequate compensation. If you are able to describe a situation in which the company, through little or no fault of your own, will clearly not be able to keep or pay its top people what they're worth (for example: a pending merger, bankruptcy, cash flow problems, loss of a key customer or product). Clearly, your reason for leaving is obvious and justifiable, your future there dim. "Well, I doubt I'll last the week. Old Scrawnynose will probably fire me right after lunch." An answer that indicates problems at the company for which you must bear some responsibility. ("Well, sales are down 10 percent across the board but my territory is down 72 percent. It's not my fault that all those stores went out of business!") Although it's a good idea to convince your prospective employer that the world is your oyster—and you're simply waiting to find the perfect pearl of a job—you might get hit with questions like these: Q: If you're so happy at your current job, why are you leaving? Will they be surprised? What do they want to hear? You might think your current company will go out of business at any second. Or you may be leaving because you just broke off your engagement with the person in the office next door. Don't cry on the interviewer's shoulder. Instead, reassure him or her that you're not running away from anything. You've made the decision to move toward: Ö More responsibility. Ö More knowledge. Ö The wonderful opportunity available at Good Times, Inc. Variations | What would have to change at your current job to make it tenable? | What have you had to change about yourself/your skills/ philosophy/duties to adapt to changes at your current firm? | What aspects of your current job were different than you expected when you took it? Q: If you have these complaints about your current job/boss/company, and they think so highly of you, why haven't you brought your concerns to their attention? What do they want to hear? The interviewer is trying to "hoist you by your own petard." Some problem solver you are! You can't even talk to your boss about changes that might make you happier. If you do find yourself cornered, facing this dead end, the only way out is to be as positive as possible. Say something like: "Grin & Bear It is aware of my desire to move up. But the company is still small. There's really not much they can do about it. The management team is terrific. There's no need right now to add to it, and they are aware of some of the problems this creates in keeping good performers. It's something they talk about quite openly." Variations | If you could eliminate one duty/ responsibility from your current (last) job, what would it be and why? | If you could make one comment or suggestion to your current boss, what would it be? Did you do anything of the sort? Why or why not? Q: How would your coworkers describe you? What do they want to hear? Of course, they would describe you as an easygoing person who is a good team player. After all, you've found that "a lot more can be accomplished when people gang up on a problem, rather than on each other." Once again, the personal inventory you completed in Chapter 2 will come in handy. Cull words from the lists I encouraged you to make: "My strongest skills," "My greatest areas of knowledge," "My greatest personality strengths," and "The things I do best"— and put them in the mouths of coworkers and friends. Variations | What five adjectives would your last supervisor use to describe you? | How effectively did your supervisor conduct appraisals? | How did you do on your last performance appraisal? | What were your key strengths and weaknesses mentioned by your supervisor? | How did your last supervisor get the best performance out of you? | What did you say and do the last time you were right and your boss was wrong? Q: Give me specific examples of what you did at your current (last) job to increase revenues, reduce costs, be more efficient, etc. What do they want to hear? This ties in to the earlier questions you were asked about budgetary responsibility and how your current department is organized. (Savvy interviewers think it's a good idea after asking the first question or two to ask some different questions, then return to the subject later. Many candidates, having successfully navigated the shoals of the earlier questions, may be caught in an exaggeration when the interviewer returns to the question later on rather than following it up immediately.) Q: What do you feel an employer owes an employee? What do they want to hear? This is not—let me repeat, not—your invitation to discuss the employee benefits package you would like to have. It's a loaded question. Don't get into a dissertation on the employer's moral or legal responsibility to employees. Try to refocus the interviewer's attention on your positive outlook, and keep your answer short and sweet: "I think an employer owes its employees opportunity. In my next position, I look forward to the opportunity to run projects profitably." If the interviewer digs for a more specific response about a sensitive issue—such as your feelings about the information an employer should share with employees or the size of the raise pool—you could respond like this: I hope that my employer will be respectful of me as an employee and of any agreements we may negotiate in the course of business. However, I know that there are times when organizations face tough decisions that may require confidentiality and affect employees. That's business." Q: The successful candidate for this position will be working with some highly trained individuals who have been with the company for a long time. How will you mesh with them? What do they want to hear? Your answer should indicate your eagerness—as the new kid on the block—to learn from your future coworkers. You don't want to raise any doubts about how they might react to you. So convey the fact that, while you are certainly bringing something to the party (skills, knowledge, your own insights), you realize you have a lot to learn from the people you'll be working with (even if, in your heart of hearts, you think they're probably a bunch of old fogies and can't wait to get on board and shape them up). Q: Your supervisor tells you to do something in a way you know is dead wrong. What do you do? What do they want to hear? This is a tough question, so why not acknowledge it with an answer like this: "In a situation like this, even the best employee runs the risk of seeming insubordinate. I would pose my alternative to my supervisor in the most deferential way possible. If he insisted that I was wrong, I guess I'd have to do it his way." Q: If you were unfairly criticized by your supervisor, what would you do? What do they want to hear? All of us can think back to a time when the pressure was on at work and a mistake was made. Maybe you took more than your fair share of the blame. Perhaps you were caught in circumstances beyond your control. In any event, your boss blamed you. But chances are, you and your boss got through the rough spot and you made sure the mistake never occurred again. You could answer the question by telling of such an experience. You do not have to select the most vulnerable or perilous moment of your career to illustrate the point. Simple mistakes are more than adequate: "In the course of my career there have been a few times when problems have come up and I have been held accountable for mistakes I did not feel I had caused. But a problem is a problem no matter who creates it, and you certainly don't have to create the problem to solve it. The most important thing is to deal with it. "On those occasions when the issue has been significant enough, I have explained my point of view to my supervisor later—after the situation has been resolved and the atmosphere has calmed." Q: Would you like to have your boss's job? Why or why not? What do they want to hear? No matter how you answer this question, the interviewer will learn a lot about you, so proceed with caution. It's an indirect way of finding out whether or not you want to be promoted. Let's start with the first part of the question: Saying "yes" indicates you're ambitious and interested in career advancement. Saying "no" indicates doubts or reservations, at least about the job in question. In the second part of the question, things get sticky. For instance, if it's clear that you're interested in promotion and the position you are applying for doesn't offer a direct path to a higher level, then the interviewer may conclude that you'll be disappointed. On the other hand, in a highly competitive organization, expressing reservations about career advancement could knock you out of the running immediately. There are two things you should do to prepare for this question. First, in your preliminary research, get a sense of the corporate culture and opportunities for advancement. Try to be aware of the possibilities going into the interview. Second, identify your honest answer to the question. Maybe you're ready, willing, and anxious to move up and take on your boss's job. Or maybe you shudder at the thought of a management job where you have to deal with personnel issues. "Know thyself" on this one, because if you're hired, your answer may come back to haunt you. Now put the results together to develop your response. Ideally, your honest answer will suit the company. If your aspirations are incompatible with the possibilities, you can—at your own risk—compensate by offering an answer that fits. No matter what, make it positive: "In time, I would love to have my boss's job. I'm particularly interested in the vendor relationships and sales promotion sides of buying." "I am very interested in career advancement, but my current boss's responsibilities are heavily weighted toward managing department production. In time, I hope to move into a position with primary responsibility for design quality." "I would be open to taking on additional responsibilities, but I like the autonomy of a sales position, and I find it rewarding to work directly with clients. My boss is mainly responsible for supervising the department and its personnel. In such a position, I would miss the client contact."

Q: Please tell me a joke Please don't. This is the only example I am going to include of questions that are, for lack of a better term, stupid. I personally don't care what kind of tree you think you are, what animal represents your management style, or what your zodiacal sign means, and neither should any other interviewer. But, of course, some of them do. So treat any such question—or a disconcerting suggestion like "tell me a joke"—as the unwelcome diversion that it is. Find a way to bring the conversation back to the particulars you know you need to emphasize and the traits and skills you need to feature. Oh, and don't tell them a joke. But you can always craft an answer that discusses how a sense of humor is an important attribute when diffusing a volatile situation, along with a pertinent example.

9

So Why Us?

In most prizefights, the first couple of rounds are relatively boring. The boxers spend their time checking each other out— assessing each other's feints and jabs—before the real mayhem begins. The same could be said of most interviews. After the first bell, the pleasantries begin. The second bell signals the "gettingto-know-you" round of questioning. Then, if the interviewer thinks it's worthwhile, he begins "pummeling" you with questions meant to separate the "stiffs" from the real contenders. If you've already confidently answered a dozen or so questions, you're in that pummeling stage. Your chance to dance around open-ended questions is long gone. In order to make it to the final bell, you need to demonstrate some real knowledge. Q: What do you know about our company? What do they want to hear? Believe it or not, many candidates think this is merely an icebreaker and simply answer, "Nothing, really." Don't follow suit! After all, why would you go into one of the most important encounters of your life so thoroughly unprepared? And then admit it? I have urged (okay, nagged) you to do your homework. This is where your research will come in handy. Toss out a few salient (and positive) facts about the company, and finish by lobbing a question that demonstrates your interest back into the interviewer's court. For example: "Boy, what a growth story Starter Up is! Didn't I read recently that you've had seven straight years of double-digit growth? I read in your annual report that you're planning to introduce a new line of products in the near future. I jumped at the chance to apply here. Can you tell me a little bit about this division and the position you're interviewing for?" Any answer that demonstrates your pre-interview research. The more informed you are, the more likely you should end up at the top of the list of potential employees. A detailed answer that indicates the breadth of your research, from checking out the company's Internet site to reading its annual report and being familiar with its products and services. Referring to a trade magazine article that mentions the company or, better yet, the interviewer, is a nice touch, don't you think? Variations | What are the most important trends you see in our industry? | What do you think are our best products or services? | How do you think our major competitors are doing? By the way, who are they? | What do you know about the community (town, city) in which we're located? | In which of our offices would you prefer to work? | Would you have a problem traveling between a few of our offices? Q: Do you have any questions? What do they want to hear? In a traditionally structured interview, this question occurs very near the end of the interview. In fact, you may well assume that its appearance signals that end. If you are unsure of whether you want a particular job, there is nothing wrong with letting the interviewer take the reins and direct the conversation. Through her questioning, you will probably get a much clearer understanding of what exactly she is looking for...and whether that "person" is you (or whether you want to be that person). But do you have to wait until the interviewer puts you through the wringer, smiles benevolently, and actually asks, "So, do you have any questions?" I really don't think so, especially if you have decided it is a job you want and are qualified for, in which case I would be more assertive and start asking your own questions. Just keep a couple of caveats in mind. First and foremost, always ask permission to ask the first couple of questions. Once it's clear the interviewer has no problem with your asking questions even as she continues to pepper you with her own, you will have established some easy rapport and won't need to ask permission each time. But it's up to you to make sure the interviewer is comfortable with your approach. If he shows obvious signs of discomfort—frowning while saying okay, pursing his lips, or showing in any other way that he clearly is not too keen on your interrupting his supposedly well-crafted approach to the interview session—back off! But if an interviewer suggests you are free to ask questions at any time or tells you it's fine when you ask permission, do so! In that case, waiting for the ubiquitous "Do you have any questions?" is a bad move: The interviewer may have already downgraded you because you didn't take her (strong) hint to be assertive right from the start.

Asking questions during the regular interview does not mean interrupting. And it doesn't mean always answering an interviewer's question with a question of your own, which may well thwart the interviewer's attempts to assess your strengths. Taking the initiative and asking questions early (with the interviewer's permission, of course) is the scenario I prefer, both as an interviewee and an interviewer. As an interviewer, it impresses me. It makes me believe (barring evidence to the contrary) that the person in front of me is interested, engaged, and assertive. As an interviewee, I want to exert some control of the interview—subtly steering it in the direction I want it to go—and asking questions early and often certainly accomplishes that. Doing so is especially effective with an inept (or at least less-than-veteran) interviewer, who may welcome your help. Another great reason to ask questions early and often is because it transforms a stilted, traditional "Q & A"—with you being the "A"—into a conversation. By definition, this makes the meeting less formal, less "you vs. me," more "we." And a conversation is how you explore areas of common interest, trade comments, chat rather than "talk." In other words, it's the way you establish the personal chemistry that is one of the vital factors in landing any job! Once the applicant pool has been whittled down to a select two or three candidates, there is usually little difference between their qualifications. What differentiates one from another may well be the relationships established during the interview process...and the interviewers' assessments of how each candidate will fit in. Last but not least, asking a good question is a slick way to sidestep an uncomfortable question from the interviewer (at least, for the time being). How do you explain that one-year gap in your resume? Darn. You didn't want to have to talk about that aborted dot-com bomb yet. Don't expect the topic to die. You are, at best, buying a temporary reprieve, but at least you've given yourself a little time to think about how you want to defuse a potentially uncomfortable situation. By interspersing your own smart questions throughout the interview, when the interviewer finally asks, "Do you have any (other) questions?" to signal the end of the interview, you may well be able to reply, "No, not really, I think we've covered all the bases." And you wouldn't have to worry that she will reject you for a lack of interest...since you have clearly demonstrated your interest throughout the interview. What do you want to know? It's easy to get caught up in the challenge of impressing the interviewer with your brilliant answers, but it's also important that you don't lose sight of the fact that you have a goal—trying to determine whether this situation is right for you, whether this job is worthy of your talents and commitment. With this in mind, here are a few key questions I would want to ask: "Can you give me a formal, written description of the position? I'm interested in reviewing in detail the major activities involved and what results are expected." This is a good question to pose to the screening interviewer. It will help you prepare to face the hiring manager. If a written description doesn't exist, ask the interviewer to dictate as complete a description of the job to you as possible. "Does this job usually lead to other positions at the company? Which ones?" You don't want to find yourself in a dead-end job. So find out how you can expect to advance after you land this job. What happened to the person you would be replacing? Is he or she still with the company? If so, doing what?Try to pursue this line of questioning without giving the impression that you can't wait to get out of a job you don't even have yet! If you ask in a completely nonthreatening manner, your ambition will be understood, even welcomed. "Tell me some of the particular skills or attributes that you want in the candidate for this position." The interviewer's answer should tell you how much your traits are valued. With this information, you can underline those traits you possess at the close of the interview to end it on a strong note. "Please tell me a little bit about the people with whom I'll be working most closely." I wish someone had told me about this question before my last job interview! The answer can tell you so many things, like how good the people you could be working with are at their jobs and how much you are likely to learn from them. Most important, you'll find out whether the hiring manager seems enthusiastic about his team. A hiring manager usually tries to put on his best face during an interview, just as you do as the prospective candidate. But catching the interviewer off guard with this question can give you a glimpse of the real feelings hiding behind the "game face." If she doesn't seem enthusiastic, you probably won't enjoy being part of the team. This particular hiring manager may attribute little success, and perhaps a lot of headaches, to the people who work for her. "What do you like best about this company? Why?" If the interviewer hems and haws a lot over this one, it may indicate that she doesn't really like the company that much at all. If she's instantly enthusiastic, her answer should help sell you on her and the company. The answer to this question can also give you a good sense of the values of the organization and the hiring manager. If she talks about nothing but products and how well her stock options are doing, it indicates a lack of enthusiasm for the people side of the business. "What is the company's ranking within the industry? Does this position represent a change from where it was a few years ago?" You should already have some indication of the answer to this question from your initial research, particularly if the company is publicly owned. If you have some of this information, go ahead and build it into your question: "I've read that the company has risen from fifth to second in market share in just the past three years. What are the key reasons for this dramatic success?" This question again clearly illustrates that you have done your research...and are ready to flaunt it! Avoid asking about days off, vacation, holidays, sick pay, personal days, and so on, at least until the interviewer has actually offered you the job. You'll seem like someone who is looking for a chance to get out of the office before you even start! Here's a list of questions to ask about the company, department, and job itself. While you should attempt to answer as many as you can before the interview, this will not always be possible, especially if you are interviewing with a small, privately held company.

Questions about the company

Ö Are you currently planning any acquisitions? Ö Do you have a lot of employees working flextime or telecommuting? Ö How rapidly is the company growing? Ö How many employees work for the organization?

Ö Is there anything else you feel it is vital I know about the company (or department, job, expectations, and so on)? Ö On a scale of 1 to 10, how would you rate the work environment here in terms of stress (congeniality, workload, teamwork, and so on)? Ö Please explain the company's organizational chart. Ö What are the company's strengths and weaknesses? Ö What are your goals for the next few years? Ö What are your key markets? Are they growing? Ö What are your leading products or services? Ö What are your prospects and plans for growth and expansion? Ö What do you like best about this company? Why? Ö What do you see as key goals for the company during the next year? Ö What growth rate are you currently anticipating? Will this be accomplished internally or through acquisitions? Ö What has been your layoff history in the last five years? Do you anticipate any cutbacks in the near future? If you do, how will they impact my department or position? Ö What is your hiring philosophy? Ö What is your ranking within the industry? Does this represent a change from where it was a year or a few years ago? Ö What is your share of each of your markets? Ö What major problems or challenges have you recently faced? How were they addressed? What results do you expect? Ö What products or services are you planning to introduce in the near future? Ö Which other company serving your markets pose a serious threat? Ö Who owns the company?

Ö Will you be entering any new markets in the next couple of years? Which ones and via what types of distribution channels?

Questions about the department

Ö Are there specific challenges you are facing right now? Ö Can you tell me about a successful project and how you managed it? Ö Can you tell me about some recent problems you've faced and how you (as a team) overcame them? Ö Can you explain the organizational structure of the department and its primary functions and responsibilities? Ö How is the department's performance measured? Ö How many people work exclusively in this department? Ö If you could change one thing about the way this department works (or is structured, managed, compensated, and so on), what would it be? Ö To whom does my boss report? Ö To whom will I be reporting? Ö What are the department's specific objectives for the next three months? Ö What are the department's strengths and weaknesses? Ö What are the departments current goals and objectives? Ö What has the turnover been in this department in the last couple of years? Ö What is the department's budget? Who is part of the planning process? Ö What was the last great challenge faced by the department? How did you and your team handle it? Ö What would you most like to see changed in this department? Ö With which other departments would I work most closely?

Questions about the job Ö Are there a lot of after-hours business events I will be expected to attend? Ö Are there other things you would like someone to do that are not considered "formal" parts of the job? Ö Can you give me a better idea of the kinds of decisions I could make (or amounts of money I could spend) without oversight? Ö Could you describe a typical day in this position? Ö Does this job usually lead to other positions in the company? Which ones? Ö How advanced or current is the hardware and software I will be expected to use? Ö How did this job become available? Was the previous person promoted? What is his or her new title? Was the previous person fired? Why? Ö How do you see me working with each of the department heads? Ö How do you see my role evolving in the first two years? Ö How has this job been performed in the past? Ö How long has this position been available? Ö How many hours per week do you expect your star employees to put in? Ö How many people will be reporting to me? Ö How much budgetary responsibility would I have? Ö How much day-to-day autonomy would I have? Ö How much discretion would I have to hire my own people? Ö How much input would I have in determining my team's or department's goals, objectives and deadlines? Ö How much travel should I expect to do in a typical month? Ö How will we work together to establish objectives and deadlines in the first months of this job?

Ö How would my performance be measured? Ö Is a written job description available? Ö Is relocation an option, a possibility, or a requirement? Ö Is there anyone within the organization who is interviewing for this position? Ö On a scale of 1 to 10, how would you rate a successful candidate's chance to advance from this position? Ö On what basis are raises and bonuses awarded? Ö Please tell me a little bit about the people with whom I'll be working most closely. Ö Please tell me more about your training programs. Do you offer reimbursement for job-related education? Time off? Ö What are three specific goals I should set for my first three months on the job? Ö What three things need immediate attention? Ö What do you think my biggest challenge will be? Ö What is the first problem I should tackle? Ö What is the one thing I should do during my first three months on the job? Ö What kind of training should I expect and for how long? Ö What skills are in short supply here? Ö What will my days be like? Ö What would be the most logical areas for me to evolve into? Ö What would you like to be able to say about your new hire one year from now? Ö Where will I be working? May I see it? Ö Would I be able to speak with the person who held this job previously? Ö Would I be able to unilaterally fire an underperforming team member?

Q: What interests you most about this position? Our company? What do they want to hear? You know the drill from some of the previous chapters: You have your eye on more responsibility, more opportunities, the chance to supervise more people, and the chance to develop a new set of skills and sharpen the ones you've already acquired. And, of course, if they absolutely insist they'll increase your salary, well, you certainly aren't one to be negative and say no! However, this is also the ideal time to show what you know about this company and how the position you're interviewing for can contribute to its success. C| Armed with this knowledge, you might reply: "I've heard so much about your titanium ball bearings that I've wanted to experiment with different applications for them." Rather than, "I'll have a better commute if I get this job." (Unbelievably, I have heard this response from more than one candidate I've interviewed! It may be honest, even important to the candidate, but it sure wasn't the answer I wanted to hear.) Be careful of any answer that clearly demonstrates incompatibility. If your primary interest lies in an area that will be peripheral, at best, to your real function, you're just setting yourself up for a "thank you, we'll be in touch." Variation | On a scale of one to five, rate your interest in this company. In this job. Q: What have you heard about our company that you don't like? What do they want to hear? This is tricky. Obviously you want to minimize the negative implications of any question, including this one. If there hasn't been any dire news, you could ask about the dearth of the most recent software or your wish that the company's profits were a bit more predictable.

Of course, the existence of real news changes your response. Maybe you've heard that ABC Widget had a layoff 12 months ago and you're wondering if the dust has settled yet. Or perhaps you've heard rumors of a merger. Don't play dumb. Given either of the above scenarios, any new prospect would have reservations about the company's stability and plans for the future. If the interviewer opens the door for you to ask what might otherwise be uncomfortable questions, by all means walk right in. Just don't slam the door in your own face by raising a huge negative: "I'm not sure I like the fact that I'll be reporting to three different executives" or "Is it possible to be scheduled for a salary review in 30 days?" Q: This is a much larger (smaller) company than you've worked for. How do you feel about that? What do they want to hear? If the company is larger, you are undoubtedly looking forward to terrific growth opportunities and exposure to more areas of knowledge than you have access to now. If the prospective company is smaller, you are looking forward to a far less bureaucratic organization, where decisions can be made much more quickly and where no department is so large that its people are unfamiliar with the workings of the entire company. Q: What are you looking for in your next job? What do they want to hear? Obviously, you should tailor your response to the job you're applying for. But answering with a slightly reorganized rendition of the job description isn't the right way to go about it. Interviewers typically ask a question like this to gauge your level of interest in the job and see if you have any doubts. So focus on the job at hand. Think of key skills the job requires and emphasize your interest in having a chance to develop (or further develop) one of them. And don't forget to express enthusiasm for your field of work. Here is an example: "In my current position as development research associate, I research corporate and government funding opportunities and write grant proposals. I enjoy my work very much, but my contact with prospective donors has been limited. I look forward to a position that offers more opportunities to work with donors, securing their support, and insuring that they are recognized for their contributions. "I have had a few opportunities to do this with my current employer, and based on my success in dealing with Timely Donations, Inc., I know I can successfully advocate an organization's mission to gain needed corporate support." Variations | If you could have any job in the world, what would it be? | If you could work for any company in the world, which would it be? | Describe your ideal job. This is not the time to wax philosophical about your dreams, let alone your fantasies. You may well harbor a desire to work in Paris, but if the company with which you're interviewing doesn't happen to have an office in France, why are you bothering to bring it up? On the other hand, disingenuously telling the interviewer that his is your dream company is not usually believable. Since virtually any answer is just going to land you in the proverbial hot water, you'd do better to find a way to slide around the question as quickly as possible. Q: Please describe the job for which you are applying. Is there a distinct difference between what you think you are going to be doing and what the interviewer has assumed are your major duties? Then this question will undoubtedly reveal them. If a disparity becomes obvious, make sure you take the time to cite examples that illustrate the competencies or experience you now know are required. Q: What aspect of the job I've described appeals to you least? What do they want to hear? Let me lead with a little humor. After conversing with his Irish friend one day, a man finally blurted out in consternation, "Why do the Irish always answer a question with a question?" Unruffled, the Irishman winked and replied, "Do we, now?" Your best tactic is to follow suit. Shoot the question right back at the interviewer! For example, you might say: "You've described a position in which I'd be overseeing some extraordinary levels of output. What sort of quality control procedures does this company have? Will I be able to consult with in-house specialists?" Much like the question asked earlier ("What have you heard about our company that you don't like?"), I would presume this question is inviting a real answer. If you aren't going to take the job (unbeknownst to the interviewer) because of what you believe to be a fundamental flaw in the job or the company, a good interviewer will want to know about it. One of three possible scenarios will result: Ö You'll reveal an invalid or mistaken objection. Once the interviewer answers it, you will again be an interested candidate. Ö You'll reveal a viable objection that leads the interviewer to eliminate you from consideration. Ö You'll reveal a viable objection that will lead you to remove yourself from consideration.

Q: Based on what you know about our industry, how does your ideal job stack up against the description of the job for which you're applying? What do they want to hear? The "ideal" job is always one in which you'll have a broad scope of responsibilities that will enable you to continue to learn about your industry and grow. So use your knowledge about the industry to formulate a reply that, though perhaps a bit idealistic, doesn't sound unrealistic: "I know that many accounting firms are deriving more and more of their fee income from consulting services. I'd like a job that combines my cost accounting knowledge with client consultation and problem solving. Ideally, I'd like to start as part of a team, then eventually head up a practice in a specific area, say, cost accounting in manufacturing environments." Now, based on what you know about the position, touch on one (and only one) minor shortcoming, and formulate a few careful questions about some aspects of the position you don't know about. Expanding on the above example, you might say: "I know this position is in the auditing area and that you hire many of your entry-level people into that department. I must confess, I would like this to be a stepping stone to working more in the manufacturing area and, several years down the line, in consulting. I'm sure I don't have the requisite knowledge or experience yet. Is this a position in which I can gain such experience, and is this a career track that's possible at this firm?" Q: How will you handle the least interesting or most unpleasant parts of this job? What do they want to hear? An interviewer posing this question usually will build in specific aspects of the position, such as: "You won't always be looking for creative solutions to our clients' tax problems. Most of the time, you'll be churning out returns and making sure you comply with the latest laws. You're aware of that, of course?" You might answer: "I'm sure that every job in the accounting field has its routine tasks. They have to be done, too. Doing those tasks is part of the satisfaction of doing the job well. They make the relatively infrequent chances we have to be creative even more satisfying." Q: You've had little experience with budgeting (or sales or whatever). How do you intend to learn what you need to know to perform on this job? What do they want to hear? "Well, throughout my career, I've proven to be a quick study. For example, when my company's inventory system was computerized, I didn't have the time to go through the training. But the company that supplied the software had developed some computerbased tutorials and training manuals. I studied them and practiced at home. I hope that I'd be able to do something similar to pick up the rudiments of your budgeting system." You could also mention other options, such as learning from professional publications and seminars. Show your initiative and resourcefulness in getting up to speed quickly. The interviewer wants to be sure you won't just be sitting around twiddling your thumbs and complaining that you don't know what to do next. Reassure him or her that you plan to do whatever it takes to go right on learning throughout your tenure. Now, how would you step in and save the day? If you don't know as much as you'd like to about the position for which you're interviewing, spend some time with industry and trade publications. Focus on articles written to help people in this type of position solve common problems—or that suggest tips, tricks, and tools designed to increase everyday efficiency .

You want to demonstrate that you're ready to step right in and handle a tough situation with a cool head. It's also a good idea to sharpen your working knowledge and skills. Interviewers like to pose problems you can solve on the spot. These exercises are intended to demonstrate your proficiency in the areas most important to the job. Preparation makes perfect. If you come up blank, or use a fact or formula inaccurately during one of these exercises, it will be difficult, if not impossible, to recoup your credibility. That would be especially unfortunate after you've gotten this far. Caveat: Different companies may use slightly different terms for the same procedure or material. So explain your terminology up front to make sure you're communicating clearly. Q: How long do you plan to stay with us? What do they want to hear? One answer I don't want to hear is "forever," because I simply won't believe it (and I'll wonder about the intelligence of a candidate who would think that's what I want to hear). You should offer a fairly simple answer along the lines of "as long as I continue to grow, continue to learn, and continue to contribute in ways you feel are valuable." I'm not sure whether this question will ever give an interviewer any useful information, because any candidate candid (or stupid) enough to answer "oh, a month or two, until I find a job I really like" shouldn't have made it through the screening process (or, for that matter, the first two questions of the interview). But be careful your body language doesn't reveal your real answer. Squirming does imply, "Oh, a month or two, until I find a job I really like!" If you already appear to be a job-hopper but trot out the standard "as long as I continue to grow" speech, don't be surprised if the interviewer asks, "Is that what you told the interviewers at your four previous positions?" Whatever you do, don't answer, "Yep, and they all believed me, too!"

Q: How do you think I've handled this interview? What do they want to hear? Well, your options aren't very pleasant, are they? Saying "lousy" doesn't seem appropriate, but "great, sir, and may I polish your shoes?" seems a bit too obsequious. There is no right answer, so don't offer one—ask a question of your own instead: "I think your questions have given me a good opportunity to discuss many of my strengths and qualifications already. What else can I tell you to convince you I am absolutely the best candidate for this job?" Variations | How well do you think I've conducted this interview so far? | Am I talking too much? | What do you think of the questions I've asked so far?

10

Questions About Your Personal Life

Most people think that the candidate who talks only about work, work, work stands the best chance of getting the job. But there's a "you" that exists after 5 p.m.—and most interviewers want to get to know that person, too. The guiding principle for answering personal questions is the same as it is for responding to queries about your professional experiences: Emphasize the positive. Let the interviewer in on the best and most interesting aspects of your personality. Just be careful of saying too much. Your answers can reveal more information than the interviewer is entitled by law to ask for. For example, in the warm glow of an interview that seems to be going well, you might feel comfortable talking about your children and the challenges of being a single parent. The interviewer could not have asked about your family situation in order to eliminate you from the running. Yet once this information is out, it's fair game. He or she is free to use it to make unfair judgments about your ability to handle various aspects of the job. If the job you're applying for involves occasional overnight travel, for example, he or she may decide your family situation would create unnecessary difficulties. So, while these questions do give you an opportunity to demonstrate what a terrific person you are, they could also prompt you to—unwittingly—provide information that does you in as a prospective candidate for employment! A little later in this chapter, I will help you identify questions that are, at best, inappropriate and, at worst, illegal. When does the interview actually start? As the head of recruiting for a rather large company, a friend of mine spent weeks at a time interviewing scores of candidates for a wide variety of openings. With so much practice, she became very good at identifying unsuitable candidates in minutes—and "releasing" the unsuspecting person with a simple, "Thanks for stopping by" before the interview even got underway! Here's how it worked: On greeting a young applicant for a field sales position one morning, my friend asked, "How are you?" The applicant immediately began whining that it was raining and she had a run in her stocking. My friend turned to her and, feigning embarrassment, said, "Oh! Are you here to apply for that field sales position? I'm sorry. We forgot to call. We filled the position yesterday. But we'll keep you in mind for other, similar positions that come along. Thanks for stopping by." This story demonstrates a fact that few candidates realize: There is no such thing as an innocent or "throwaway" question. You are being judged from the moment the interviewer sees you (or hears you on the telephone) until the instant you are offered the job (or escorted out of the building). Many interviewers use these questions as icebreakers, believing that they give a false, informal impression of "let's just chat, shall we?" and lead candidates to drop their interview guard. Some interviewees, dismissed after only a few minutes, belatedly discover that these innocent questions "ice-picked" their chance for the job. Following are just a few to be prepared for Q: How are you today? What do they want to hear? You're doing just fine, thank you. And no, you didn't have any trouble at all finding their offices. That's because (don't admit to this, just do it) you took the time to get directions from the interviewer's assistant. Again, it all comes down to being positive. I'm not suggesting that you plaster an idiot grin on your face and go on like a "Stepford" employee. But I do urge you to make every effort not to let anything negative (even the crummy weather) enter into any part of your interaction with the interviewer. Since my recruiter friend told me her little story, I know I pay much more attention to the answers candidates give to these little throwaway questions. Variations | Did you have any trouble finding us? | Where are you staying? Do you like the hotel? | How was your flight? Q: What's the last book you read? What do they want to hear? What someone chooses to read speaks volumes about what kind of a person he or she is. But before you reel off your reading list, consider this: Right or wrong, many interviewers seem to think that people who read nonfiction are more interested in the world about them than fiction readers, whom they may believe are looking for an escape. So rather than talk about the latest thriller you couldn't put down, opt for a popular how-to book. This will demonstrate that you're interested in The 7 Habits of Highly Effective People or The Discipline of Market Leaders, or generally trying to improve your knowledge and skill as a businessperson.

Q: What's the last movie you saw? What do they want to hear? Mention a popular but noncontroversial movie. It won't do you any good to gleefully admit it was Friday the 13th, Part 86. Do you want your taste in foreign films or left-wing documentaries to stand between you and a job? If you insist your preferences shouldn't matter, feel free to discuss them. Variations | What three people would you most like to have dinner with? | What other person would you invite to a desert island? | What's your favorite book? | Who's your favorite author? | Who's your favorite actor? | What's your favorite movie? | What's your favorite TV show? | What magazines do you read regularly? | Where do you get your news? | Tell me a favorite quote. Q: If I went on to your Facebook page right now, what would I find? Everyone has been telling you for years that anything posted online never dies, so of course you never put photos of yourself with drink in hand (or face on floor). Wait. You did? What were you thinking? Okay, but you deleted them before you started your job search, right? NO? WHAT WERE YOU THINKING? The older the interviewer, the less likely he is intimately involved with social media, though this is just a generalization. But many companies are now routinely checking applicants' Facebook pages, Twitter feeds, blogs, and other social media sites, so have the good sense to scrub yours clean. And be prepared for questions about your Internet presence you wouldn't have faced even a few years ago.

Variations | How many friends do you have on Facebook? | What's your favorite website? | What's your favorite podcast? | Who do you follow on Twitter? | How many Twitter followers do you have? | What's your favorite blog? | What's the most-used app on your phone? | How much time do you spend on social media sites during a typical day? Q: How do you manage to balance career and family? What do they want to hear? Gosh, you are facing one tricky devil. Again, this is a perfectly legal question, but it does make it decidedly difficult if you are determined to keep any discussion of family out of the interview. Why would you want to avoid such a discussion? If you've been around the block a few times, you may legitimately worry that the interviewer has some unwritten rules, such as no single parents hired for travel positions. Accordingly, if you're attempting to give an answer that is as unrevealing as possible, try something like this: "I have been a dedicated, loyal, hard-working employee throughout my career and nothing in my personal life—family obligations, hobbies, or volunteer work—has ever affected my performance. Nor would I ever expect it to." Q: What do you like to do when you're not at work? What do they want to hear? Many employers subscribe to the theory, "If you want something done, give it to a busy person." So, you want to portray yourself as an active, vital individual. Take this opportunity to paint a self-portrait of a well-rounded, curious, and interesting person. Be sure to emphasize those activities that may complement your on-the-job duties. For example, if you're applying for a position as a bookstore manager, mentioning that you read three books a week is highly appropriate. Your addiction to helicopter skiing probably isn't (for any job!). Variations | What are your hobbies? | What turns you on in your off-hours? | What did you do last weekend? | Where did you go on your last vacation? | So, what do you spend your extra money on? Shy away from the controversial. A savvy candidate will cite reading and tennis, for example, rather than bungee jumping, picketing abortion clinics, or raising money for the Liberal Party. Do you really want your off-hours interests to come between you and the job you're after? Then don't brag about activities that would cause a squeamish employer to envision a prolonged sick leave or a conservative one to shudder at your radical views. It's generally safe to talk about most sports activities—participating in team sports; coaching children; or indulging in singular activities such as swimming, running, walking, or bicycling. Avoid emphasizing activities that are likely to spark concern or controversy, such as sky diving or hunting. As a rule, employers like activities that show you are communityminded and people-oriented. Your involvement with the chamber of commerce, Toastmasters, Rotary Club, or fundraising for charities is likely to earn points. However, consider avoiding any religious or political activities that may alienate the interviewer. Carefully craft your answer so you don't: Sound like a couch potato. "I'm a Giants fan. I never miss a game. I also catch every rerun of my 14 favorite shows." Seem headed for a collapse. "I play racquetball, coach a softball team, am on the board of directors of the local museum, plan to run for city council this fall, and, in my spare time, attend lectures on Egyptology at the university." (And exactly where will you find the time and energy for work?) Boast about dangerous activities. "I like to challenge myself. Next weekend, I'm signed up for another parachute jump. I need something to keep me pumped up until rugby season starts." Bring up controversial interests that may be personally objectionable to the interviewer. "I'm always on the front lines at Greenpeace demonstrations." Or, "I give all my money to the Crusade to Convert the World to (fill-in-the-blank) religion." To your good health Employers have more than just a passing interest in your health. Most companies are looking for ways to keep the overall cost of health-care insurance from skyrocketing. Most managers want to know that you won't be felled by every flu bug that makes the rounds—and on sick leave when they need you most. Here are two legal questions they can ask: Q: Are you in good health? What do you do to stay in shape? You must be honest in answering this one. Prospective employers can find ways to check your medical history if they're worried about your health. In fact, many employers make job offers contingent on your passing a physical examination. If you appear to be dedicated to maintaining your own good health, you'll ease many of their concerns. You don't have to be an exercise nut. Just play up any activities you do regularly that provide at least some health benefit, such as yard work, home repairs, even walking the dog. Q: Do you have any physical problems that may limit your ability to perform this job? If so, what accommodations would be necessary? This is a perfectly legitimate question for the interviewer to ask. So be honest. Are you applying for a job that requires a lot of data entry despite the fact that you've been waging an ongoing battle with carpal tunnel syndrome? Will you be doing a lot of walking and standing on the job that might trigger that problem knee? Remember, though, the key words are "ability to perform this job." A physical problem that is not job-related is not pertinent... and none of the employer's business, by law. Discriminate and eliminate? In an ideal world, companies and managers would judge every applicant solely on the basis of the skills and experience necessary to perform the job. But it should come as no surprise that our world is far from ideal. In the real world, many managers and companies discriminate against people of color, people with disabilities, people over the age of 50, even women whom they may simply assume are planning to have children sometime during their future employment! Few of us can claim to be completely objective when judging other people. But the fact is that you, as a candidate for any job, do not have to answer questions related to your race, nationality, marital or financial status—or even a disability if it is unrelated to how well you are able to perform the job. If an interviewer is foolish enough to make an issue of your nationality, marital status, or other personal information, should you leap out of your chair and make a citizen's arrest right there in the interview? No .But you should sit up and take notice. Every state has regulations governing what may and may not be asked of an applicant during the pre-employment (application and interviewing) process. Just asking the wrong question is not illegal in itself. But it may open an employer up to a lawsuit if an otherwise-qualified applicant is passed over for a job based on his or her answer. Few companies are willing to take that chance. So when it comes to inappropriate questions, most employers tread lightly. But regulations don't preclude the subtle techniques some interviewers use to get applicants to volunteer information. As an applicant, it's still up to you to dodge the bullet. The key is knowing when a question is inappropriate—and deciding whether to surrender information that might cost you the job. Every question the interviewer asks should pass this test: Does it have something to do with your current job or the one that you're applying for? Beyond that, it pays to check with your state's Fair Employment Practices Commission for a list of questions considered inappropriate for employers to ask on job applications and during preemployment interviews. In the meantime, here are some questions that should trigger alarms in your head during even the most congenial interview. Q: How old are you? Age can be a loaded issue for many employers. If you're in your late 40s or 50s, some employers may worry about your energy flagging or your health failing. Don't give them ammunition in the form of a number. Employers cannot ask for your birth date or about facts that might reveal your age, such as the year you graduated from high school. Interviewers may only state that hiring is subject to verification of legal minimum age requirements and that employees under the age of 18 must provide a work permit. (So asking whether you are at least 18 years old is a legal question.)

But age, like race, can be easy to guess. So again, take a positive tack. Play up the benefits of your experience and assure the employer that you have all the vitality for work you had when you were in your 20s. You might say: "The more I've accomplished, the more effective I've become. When I was just starting out, I was so full of energy I was like a loose cannon. Now I find I can accomplish more in less time because I know where to find the resources I need and how to work effectively with all kinds of people." Variations | When were you born? | When did you graduate from high school? | When did you graduate from college? | Are you near retirement age? | Aren't you a little young to be seeking a job with this much responsibility? | Aren't you a little too old for a fast-changing company such as ours? Q: Are you single (married, separated, divorced)? Often an interviewer's bias is not overt. Many interviewers use subtle ploys designed to get you to volunteer just the information that they may use to disqualify you from the running. You may be married with children—and proud of it. But resist the temptation to whip out the latest pictures from Walt Disney

World. Why? After all, what could seem more innocent than chitchatting about your girlfriend, spouse, or kids? What's the harm in letting an employer know about your tentative plan for having a child within a year? Maybe there's no harm in it. But then again, you never know how an interviewer may interpret your answers. If you're planning to have a child within a year, for example, an interviewer may wonder whether you will begin to curtail your hours at work. If you're engaged to be married, he might assume that you will be so wrapped up in wedding plans that your attention won't be focused on the job at hand. Interviewers may not ask about your marital status or plans for marriage or for having children. If you already have children, you're not obliged to reveal their ages or the arrangements you've made for childcare. In many states, married women are not required to give an employer their maiden name—unless they've worked under another name at previous companies listed on their resume. You may be asked whether you are able and willing to relocate, to travel extensively, or to work overtime as needed (as long as the latter two questions are asked of all candidates). While these may be veiled attempts to discover whether you have a lot of family obligations—there may not actually be much travel or overtime—they are still legal questions and you will need to have answers ready. Meeting the interviewer halfway Rather than simply refusing to answer a question—and creating bad feelings between you and the interviewer—you may find it helpful to confront what you believe might be the employer's concerns about your situation. For example, if the interviewer keeps digging for information about whether you have children, or plan to, he may be concerned about your commitment to the job. You might respond by saying something like: "I sense that you are concerned about my ability to be here on a regular basis to put in the work necessary to meet deadlines. Just let me assure you that I have always been a reliable worker who's committed to getting the job done well and on time. In fact, in my last position, I was never late to work and I consistently completed all projects ahead of deadline." See? Without answering any questions about children or family plans, you addressed the real issue—the employer's concern about your commitment to your job. Variations | What do you think caused your divorce? | Why have you never married? | Were you ever married? | Do you intend to marry? | Do you live alone? | Do you have any children? | Do you prefer to be called Miss, Ms., or Mrs.? | Are you a single parent? | How many dependents are you responsible for? | Who's the boss in your family? | What kind of work does your spouse do? | How much time do you spend with your family? | What do you think makes a happy marriage? | Tell me about your children. | Do you have a good relationship with your children? | Do you have any children not living with you? | Do you live with your parents? | What childcare arrangements have you made for your children? | My darn kids seem to pick up every bug that comes around. Yours, too? | My wife (husband) hates me working on weekends. What about yours? | Do you practice birth control? | Are you pregnant? | Do you intend to have children? | Will travel be a burden on your family? | Are you a family man (woman)? Q: What's your nationality? When you meet, you can't stop an interviewer from drawing conclusions about your lineage from the color of your skin, eyes, or hair. But never surrender that information over the telephone or hand over a photograph of yourself before you accept a job. Employers may not ask about your ancestry, descent, parentage, or nationality—or that of your parents or spouse. It's okay to volunteer that you're proficient in a language other than English, but the interviewer cannot ask you how you learned to read, write, or speak those languages. Let's say your last name is "obviously" Italian. When you greet the interviewer, he remarks, "Rutigliano. That's Italian, isn't it?" What do you do? Just smile politely...and don't answer at all. It is quite possible that the interviewer meant absolutely no offense. If the interviewer still doesn't get the hint and continues to allude to your Italian heritage, you might say, "I really don't see what my ancestry has to do with my application for this job." If you try to handle the situation diplomatically, you can stay on the interviewer's "good" side. If an employer tries to pressure you into submitting a photograph of yourself to accompany your job application, simply say, "I don't have a suitable photograph available at this time. Of course, if I'm offered this job, I'd be happy to have one taken." The Federal Immigration Reform and Control Act of 1986 prohibits employers from hiring undocumented workers—people who are not properly authorized to work in this country. So confirming that you are authorized to work in the U.S. is perfectly legitimate. In fact, once you have accepted the offer, you will be required to document your right to work by providing your United States passport, a green card, or some combination of birth certificate, social security card, and driver's license.

Variations | Hmm, that's a (Italian, Greek, etc.) name, isn't it? | What language do you speak at home? | Where are your parents from? | Where were you born? | Where were your parents born? | What is your maiden name? | Is that the last name you were born with? | What languages do your parents speak? | What do your parents do? | Were your parents born in this country? | Were you born in this country? | What kind of accent is that? | What languages do you speak?* | Are you bilingual?* *These last two are legal questions if proficiency in one or more foreign languages is a requirement of the job. Q: What's your sexual orientation? "I'm sorry. I don't intend to discuss that." Variations | Are you straight? | Are you gay? | Are you a lesbian? | Do you date other men? | Do you date other women? | Do you have any roommates? | Do you live with anyone? | Do you belong to any gay or lesbian groups? | What gender is your spouse?

Q: Are you (Jewish, Christian, Buddhist, etc.)? Employers may tell you which religious holidays the company observes. But they cannot ask you for any specific information in this area. If an interviewer presses you to reveal your affiliation, simply say: "I like to keep my religious beliefs separate from my work, and I respect that right in the people with whom I work." But if you find yourself dodging too many of these bullets, maybe you should take a moment to think about whether you want to work for a supervisor who has shown himself to be ignorant and insensitive. If you don't care that he's an insensitive boob—or you desperately need the job—then don't make an issue out of his comments. It's up to you. Variations | What do you do Sunday mornings? | Can you work Friday evenings? | We're a (Christian, Jewish, Muslim) firm. Would that be a problem for you? | Are you a member of any religious group? | What religion do you practice? | Do you tithe? | Are you "born again"? | Do your children go to Sunday School? | Do your children go to Hebrew School? | Do your children attend a madrassa? | Do you sing in the church choir? | What church do you belong to? | What temple do you regularly attend? | Is there any day of the week on which you can't work?Will working on weekends be a problem for you? | What religious holidays will you need to take? | What organizations do you belong to? | Have you ever done any missionary work? Q: Do you have any physical problems? Interviewers may only ask about a physical or mental disability that will directly affect your performance on the job. Your general physical health is not fair game, although you may be asked to take a physical examination after you receive an offer. The outcome of this examination must be related to essential functions of the job, so the employer has the right to condition the offer on the results. Employers may not ask about whether you have: Ö An existing mental condition. Ö Received workers' compensation. Ö Problems with alcohol or drugs. Ö HIV, AIDS, or AIDS-related syndrome. Although new laws and regulations will likely be written, currently HIV infection, AIDS, and AIDS-related medical conditions are considered "disabilities" under the Americans with Disabilities Act. If you test positive for HIV or AIDS (or any other disability) in a pre-employment medical examination, the employer cannot use that information as grounds for withdrawing the offer, unless the extent of the illness substantially inhibits your ability to do the job or poses a reasonable threat to the safety of others in the workplace. Variations | Do you have any health problems? | How many days were you sick last year? | Do you spend a lot on prescriptions? | Can you read the fine print on this form?

How's your back? | Is your hearing good? | Were you ever denied health insurance? | Were you ever denied life insurance? | When were you last in the hospital? | When did you last consult a doctor? | Do you have a doctor you see regularly? | Are you handicapped? | Have you ever filed a worker's compensation claim? | Are you sensitive about your weight? | Are you on a diet? | Shouldn't you be on a diet? Q: What organizations do you belong to? Think carefully about your answer to this question. An employer can ask about (and should only be interested in) your membership in organizations, professional societies, or other associations considered important to your performance on the job. It's a good idea to leave out the names of any organizations that might provide "clues" to your race, religious creed, color, national origin, ancestry, gender, or disability. Q: Have you ever gone bankrupt? A prospective employer may only ask what you're currently earning. Your current or past assets, liabilities, or credit rating are not fair game. This includes whether you own a home or any information about a past bankruptcy or garnishment of wages (except when permitted by federal and state laws governing credit-related information). Again, it's wise to consult specific guidelines in your state.

Variations | Do you own or rent your home? | Do you have any outside income? | Do you earn any money from hobbies or investments? Q: What was your record in the military? If you have served in the military and want to highlight relevant skills and knowledge you gained from that experience, go ahead. But be aware that you're not required to give the dates of your military service or the type of discharge you received. A dishonorable discharge from the military or an arrest that did not result in a conviction does not mean your professional life is over. In the majority of cases, these facts should remain in your past. Be aware, however, that regulations do differ from state to state and from industry to industry. For example, under the Federal Deposit Insurance Act, banks are prohibited from hiring individuals convicted of any crime involving dishonesty or breach of trust, even if the conviction is more than seven years old. Variation | What kind of discharge did you receive from the military? Q: Have you ever been arrested? Unless you're applying for a position as a police officer or with the Department of Justice, a prospective employer is not entitled to know whether you've been arrested, unless the arrest resulted in a conviction. In some states, employers may only ask about felonies, not misdemeanors. If you have a criminal record, do some research. So what do you do? Over the past 25 years, there has been a plethora of lawsuits charging employers with discriminatory hiring practices, yet inappropriate questions still are commonly asked during interviews. This is particularly true of interviews by hiring managers, who may not be as informed as they should be about legal issues. If you're asked an inappropriate question, you have four choices: Ö You can choose to answer the question, assuming that (for now, at least) the interviewer is not being wily, merely curious. Ö You can choose to answer the question you think the interviewer is really asking. He may not really care if you have kids, for example, if you point out that travel and overtime are no problem. Ö You can make sure the interviewer is aware—oh so tactfully!—that she is treading on thin legal ice: "I'm not sure my religion is relevant to the job, but as you can see from my resume..." Ö You can end the interview. I'm presuming you would do this because the interviewer has not stopped with one question—despite your tactful warnings—but has continued to ask inappropriate questions. Why would you want to work in a company that has made it clear they discriminate? What to do after the fact If an interviewer has asked you questions not related to the job on offer, and you believe you weren't hired based on your refusal to answer or the information you did provide, you might have grounds for charging the employer with discrimination. The operative word here is "might." The burden of proof is on you. You will have to prove that the questions were asked for the purpose of discriminating among applicants. For example, if the manager asking all those questions about Italian ancestry subsequently hired another Italian, you wouldn't have much of a claim, despite the fact that you were asked inappropriate questions.

If you do think that you have grounds for a charge of discrimination, you should file your charges simultaneously with the appropriate state agency and the federal government's Equal Employment Opportunity Commission (EEOC). The EEOC generally will wait until the state agency has conducted an investigation, then conduct an investigation of its own. As you might expect, the wheels of government agencies can creak at their own slow pace. In fact, you might not hear anything for years! Even then, an agency will only determine whether there is reason to believe your charge is true. Therefore, if you are anxious for justice, you should request that the EEOC issue you a notice 180 days after you file your charge. If you're in the right If the EEOC determines that your complaint is valid, it will first attempt to mediate the dispute between you and the employer. If an agreement can't be reached, the commission will either file its own suit or issue you a letter giving you the right to sue the employer. You must file your suit within 90 days of receiving such a letter. If you win your lawsuit, don't expect to receive a colossal jury award. The most you'll probably get from the employer is the equivalent of a year's salary. One last word... None of the information or advice in this chapter should be taken as legal advice. I am not an attorney. If you feel a prospective employer is guilty of discrimination, your first step should be to contact the appropriate government agencies, as well as an attorney, to accurately assess your rights and options under federal law and the laws and regulations in your state and industry.

q Know your rights. Do some research to find out what questions are out of bounds in your particular state, industry, or profession. q Don't open the door for the interviewer. Let him get it himself! That is, don't bring up subjects you don't want to talk about. If you do, the interviewer is likely to ask what would otherwise have been illegal questions...if you hadn't opened the door first. q Change the subject. If you feel that the interviewer is asking you questions that shouldn't be asked, the first step is to try to shrug them off and change the direction of the conversation. q Give them the benefit of the doubt. After all, you are here because you want the job. So it's up to you to weigh your personal reactions to certain searching questions against your desire to have this job. Many hiring managers may not realize they are in the wrong. Give them the benefit of the doubt. q Warn the interviewer...subtly. Tell the interviewer in a nonthreatening way that you know the questions he or she is asking are inappropriate. This should deliver the message that you know your rights and aren't willing to be a victim of discrimination. q End the interview. If the interviewer refuses to back off, end the interview quickly. After all, would you really want to work at a company or for a person capable of such narrow-minded attitudes? If you think you have a strong case, look into bringing formal charges against the company and the interviewer.

11

Questions to Wrap Things Up

Okay, you've made it this far, you must have the job by now. Anyway, there's absolutely no way to mess it up at this point, right? Don't be so quick to relax. The closing questions of an interview should be handled with care. There are still likely to be some tough questions ahead. Here goes: Q: Are you willing to travel? What do they want to hear? Yes, of course you are. Your family understands the demands of your career and is supportive when you need to spend some time away from home. Does that mean you want to be away three weeks out of four? Probably not. Unless you are unwilling to travel at all, don't let this question cost you the job. (If the job requires far more travel than you are prepared for, what are you doing on the interview? And if the heavy travel requirements are a complete shock, why didn't you learn about them beforehand?) If travel is an important part of the job, it's more likely the interviewer will ask this question early in the process, so as to immediately eliminate home-bound candidates. Q: Are you willing to relocate? What do they want to hear? If you really are, say so: "Absolutely. In fact, I would look forward to the chance to live elsewhere and experience a different lifestyle and meet new people." If you're not, say so: "Well, not unless the job is so terrific that it would be worth uprooting my family and leaving my relatives and friends. Does this position require a move? I'm obviously very interested in it, so I might consider relocating." Q: May I contact your current employer? Why do interviewers ask this question? You will probably feel like saying, "Sure, after you give me this job and I don't have to worry about getting canned because I've been out looking for another job." But you'll sound better saying: "Sure you can—after we come to an agreement. I think it's best if they hear about this from me first." Q: May I contact your references? What do they want to hear? "Of course you can." Tell the interviewer that you will get back to him or her with a list of references that afternoon or, if it is already afternoon, the very next day. Does this stalling make you seem unprepared? Shouldn't you go into the interview with the list ready to hand over to the interviewer? Frankly, in the world of interviews, stalling for a little time before giving references is SOP (standard operating procedure). The reason you want to wait is so you can tell your prospective references that a call might be coming from Mr. Krueger of Trikadekaphobia, Inc. If your references are indeed going to say wonderful things about you, they should be prepared to do so. Caveat: Employers are growing more reluctant to provide references because of a rise in the number of claims of defamation and misrepresentation. Because job references are partially privileged communications, it's a good idea to try to get an inside line on what is being said about you to a prospective employer. As an applicant, you may be able to approach a current or former employer to work out a narrative job reference that is accurate and amenable to both of you. With your consent and involvement, former employers may be more willing to discuss your strengths and weaknesses and the circumstances surrounding your departure in a positive light. Q: Is there anything else about you I should know? What do they want to hear? You might not think you have anything else left to say, but you should. This is your chance—beautifully presented on a silver platter—to close the sale. You'd be a fool to turn it down. Develop a short answer to this question, one that features your strengths, accomplishments, skills, and areas of knowledge. In other words, a great close remarkably similar to the narrative you prepared as an answer to "tell me about yourself." For example: "Mr. Krueger, I think we've covered everything. But I want to re-emphasize the key strengths that I would bring to this position: "Experience: The job I'm currently in is quite similar to this one, and I would be excited by the chance to apply what I've learned at WidgetLand to working for your company. "Management skills: I run a department almost equal in size to this one. I'm a fair and effective supervisor. "A record of success: I've won two prestigious industry awards. I would bring that creativity here. "Enthusiasm: I am very excited about the prospect of working with you here at Trikadekaphobia. When do you expect to make a decision?"

This type of answer should underline the points that you have been trying to make throughout the entire interview. By ending with a question, you ask Mr. Krueger to take some action. This is an effective selling technique that should give you a good indication of your chances of getting the job. Variations | Why should I hire you? | If you were me, would you hire you? Money talks No one likes to talk about money during an interview. It seems "indelicate," somehow. But that doesn't mean you should avoid it completely. Just remember that timing is everything. My own rule of thumb is simple: Don't discuss dollars and cents until after you've convinced the interviewer that you're the best person for the job. That's why I've relegated the first question on salary to near the end of the final chapter. Until you've made it over all the other interview hurdles, the interviewer is still assessing your ability. And he or she is probably still seeing other contenders as well— some whose talent may come cheaper than yours. But even if an interviewer tries to pressure you into naming a specific number early in the game, avoid committing yourself. Instead, name a very broad range. You might say, "I believe a fair wage for this kind of position would be between $30,000 and $40,000." Be sure the bottom end of that range is no less than the minimum salary you would be willing to accept for the position. Once the employer has made his decision, you'll be in a much stronger bargaining position. Q: What sort of salary are you looking for? What do they want to hear? You should already have a pretty good idea of what your particular market will bear. If you don't know the high and low ends in your area (city and state) and industry, do some research. Make sure you know whether these figures represent just dollars or a compensation "package" that may include insurance, retirement programs, and other value-added benefits. If you're a woman, make sure you know what men are making doing the same job. You're bound to find a discrepancy. But you should request and expect to earn an equivalent salary, regardless of what female predecessors may have earned. Even if you've been out of a job for months, this is not the time or place to let your desperation show, so avoid gushing, "Gee, this job sounds so gosh-darned wonderful I can't believe you're going to pay me anything! Just give me an office and a phone and I'll work for the sheer fun of it!" Have confidence in your own worth. By this time, you've worked hard to sell the interviewer on your value as a future employee. Just remind her of what she's already decided. Variations | What do you think this job should pay? | What do you think you are worth? | How much do you want (expect) to make? | What are your salary expectations? | How much were you paid last year? | If I'm going to make you an offer, I want to ensure it is competitive. What will it take? Q: The salary you're asking for is near the top of the range for this job. Why should we pay you that much? What do they want to hear? Remind the employer of the cost savings and other benefits he'll enjoy when you come on board. Pull out your specifics again, if necessary. For example, you might say: "I was able to cut my previous employer's expenses by 10 percent by negotiating better deals with vendors. I think it's reasonable to expect that any additional salary we agree to would be offset by savings I could bring the company." Variations | Why are you asking for so little? | Are you willing to take a pay cut to work here? | Are you willing to take less than you made on your last job? | Do you think you were overpaid in your last position? What if you don't like their offer? If you are offered a salary close to the top of the range for that position at that company, consider it a compliment and don't think too hard about pushing for more money. You don't have that much to gain anyway, particularly in today's performancebased job market. But if you're offered a salary at the floor of the range, you may certainly consider making a case for a better deal. Never couple asking for more money with an explanation of why you need it. Rather, always couch such a request within a declaration of the "extra value" the employer should expect in return. Remind him of the cost savings and other benefits he'll enjoy when you come on board. Look for win-win solutions. If the employer is adamant about not increasing your salary, he may be amenable to a company car or some other perk that works for both of you. Unless you become overheated and frantic, employers will not be put off by your attempts to negotiate. You will not lose the offer just because you try to get a better deal—your willingness (or unwillingness) to do so may actually be the final test! Even if you're disappointed, but have decided to take the job, make sure everything ends on a friendly note. Otherwise, you're leaving a bad impression, and may be put under the microscope or on a short leash right from the start.

If you become too intransigent, you may even force them to change their minds! After all, you're already showing them you're not a team player by not giving an inch on anything, no matter how inconsequential. And don't forget that they are offering a compensation package, not just a salary. So even if you are an entry-level candidate, analyze the entire value of that package before making any decision. Some companies provide very generous benefits packages— including stock options, dental care, company cars, free lunches, and more—even to the rank and file. While these benefits won't fatten your take-home pay, at least you won't have to pay for them out of your own pocket. Q: Is there anything that will inhibit you from taking this job if offered? What do they want to hear? "Absolutely not." The interviewer is attempting to do everything in her power to ascertain whether you'll accept the job if offered and actually show up on the start date. But there is no way she can guarantee either. All she can hope to do is give you another opportunity to voice a previously hidden concern—too small a salary, a poor benefits package, a lousy cubicle, reporting to too many people, inadequate support, unrealistic sales or profit expectations, and so on. Variation | If I made you a great offer right now, would you accept on the spot? There's only one way to tell, Mr. Inteviewer, give it a try! This is also a good opportunity to clarify the details of any offer— vacation policy, bonuses, and so on: "I would love to accept the job right now, but can we discuss a few details first so I can compare everything with other offers I am considering?"

Q: Are you considering any other offers right now? What do they want to hear? This is another "closing" question I like to ask early in the process so I know what I'm up against. Of course, this is presuming that an honest answer is good for you, which, frankly, it probably isn't. Unless you believe the interviewer will respond positively to such an admission, you should play your cards very close to the vest. You probably gain nothing by admitting you have other irons in the fire, so why stir up the coals? I would not claim to be the most popular girl at the prom if I didn't actually have a date—don't make up offers you don't actually have. If you have no other offers, stay positive. You may consider citing other good interviews you've been on or point out that you are still very early in your job search, but in any case this would be your first choice because... Variations | Tell me about the other offers you're considering. | How does this job compare to others for which you are interviewing? Q: When can you start? What do they want to hear? If you've been laid off or fired, you can start immediately, of course. But if you're still working for someone else, you should give at least two weeks' notice to your employer, more if you are leaving a position in which you had considerable responsibility. As eager as you may be to get started on this new job, I know I don't have to remind you that it's never wise to burn bridges. You never know when you might have to cross one of them again! So be as accommodating as you can. For example, offer to help find and train your replacement. If it will be several weeks before you can assume your new responsibilities full mtime, offer to begin studying literature or files in your off hours. Or come into the office in the evening or on a weekend to meet members of the staff and begin to familiarize yourself with the lay of the land. You might even volunteer to attend a company event or seminar. Although it may reflect your true feelings about the job, saying you "aren't sure" when you can start implies to me you "aren't sure" about taking the job. Don't ever admit you can't start for several weeks because you want to take a vacation. I can empathize with someone who feels the need to "recover" from a bitter job experience before punching the clock at a new one, but there's just something that sticks in my craw about such an answer. Perhaps it's feeling that you're already putting your own needs above mine—maybe it's a real hardship for me to wait four weeks. Maybe it's my own idiosyncrasy, but I really hate to hear about someone planning a vacation before starting to work for me. Apres-interview etiquette Once you step out from under the bright lights and shake hands with the interviewer, it will probably take all the composure you can muster not to kick up your heels and run out of the office. But in your hurry, don't forget that the process is not quite over. There are a few standard rules of etiquette you should follow: Ö Ask when the hiring decision will be made. If you don't get word by then, it's perfectly acceptable to call the employer to inquire about the status of the position. Ö Write a thank-you note or email. Make it short and sweet. Thank the interviewer for taking the time to meet with you. Then restate your interest in the company and the position and find a way to remind the interviewer of how you can use your skill and experience to address one of the key requirements of the job. Type it in a business style and be sure there are no typographical or spelling errors. Ö Remember that if you met with more than one interviewer, you should send thank-you letters or emails to each person with whom you talked. Ask yourself the following questions after every interview and take notes on your answers: Ö How did it go? Ö What did they say? Ö What did you say? Ö How many people did you see? Ö How much time did you spend with each? Ö What role does each of them play? Ö Who seemed the most important? Ö Who is the hiring manager? Ö Who is the decision maker? Ö Who seems to most influence the decision? Ö Who else did you meet (secretaries, receptionists, department heads, peers, etc.)? Ö How quickly do they want to make a decision? Ö How do you stack up to your competition? Ö What objections did you have to overcome? Do you think you did so successfully? Ö How badly do you want this job? Ö What's the next step according to them? Ö What is your plan?

www.ingramcontent.com/pod-product-compliance
Lightning Source LLC
Chambersburg PA
CBHW071423130726
47996CB00013B/646